Cooper's Book of Glaze Recipes

Emmanuel Cooper

B.T.Batsford Ltd. London

Acknowledgement

The author would like to thank the many people who have helped in the preparation of this book, in particular Ann Slaughter, James Richardson and Nicky Stevenson, who mixed up tests, sorted out recipes and packed kilns. Without them this book would not have been prepared.

First published 1987
Reprinted 1992

ISBN 0 7134 4732 X

Typeset by Katerprint Typesetting Services, Oxford
and printed in Great Britain by
Billing & Sons Ltd, Worcester

for the publishers
B.T. Batsford Ltd.
4 Fitzhardinge Street
London W1H 0AH

Contents

Introduction

This is the second volume of glaze recipes for the studio potter. It continues in much the same pattern as the first book, *The Potter's Book of Glaze Recipes*, which has proved to be both clear and practical. The book provides useful recipes for a wide range of temperatures and firing conditions. There are, however, several notable differences. The first and most significant is the use of colouring slips applied under the glaze. The slips are put on to the pot before it is biscuit fired, and during the glaze firing they react with the glaze to give a seemingly endless range of fascinating textures, colours and surfaces. The second is the use of more 'categories' of glaze, classified according to temperature, offering the potter more choice, particularly at a time when, with rising fuel costs, lower temperature firings are even more attractive. The third is the use of particular photographs to illustrate specific glazes rather than particular effects. This, I am sure, will make the illustrations of greater use to the potter.

The fourth addition is the use of indexing of glazes for specific colours, effects, contents, etc. For example, a variety of glazes containing magnesium (which are usually matt, smooth, semi-opaque white or cream) can be easily found. Opaque glazes (opacified with tin oxide or zirconium) are listed, as are blue glaze, chrome pinks, nickel blue pinks etc. This will increase the potter's accessibility to the recipes and make various special effects easier to locate and experiment with.

Finally, a note has been added on the use of quick-fire kilns which have come into general production in the workshop.

As potters our first experience with glazes comes from either ready prepared glazes sold by commercial firms and mixed by experienced teachers or from glaze recipes culled from potter friends, teachers, books and magazines. From these we work out which glazes we like, what sort of glazes suit our particular requirements or taste, and concentrate on these, using them, experimenting with different glazes thicknesses, adjusting firing temperatures and trying different clays. This book of 1068 glaze recipes and glaze variations is for the potter and student who wants to start with a variety of glazes from which a wide range of effects can be developed. Some are for 'functional' use giving good, reliable, workable glazes, others offer the potter the opportunity to experiment with a range of glaze effects and decorative surfaces.

Just as the good cook starts with a recipe and then, when familiar with it, makes it 'individual', so the good potter learns how to handle, control and develop a glaze recipe. Most potters, especially when they are starting out, find the whole process of glazing very difficult. The apparently mysterious ingredients, the intricates of kiln firing and the sheer spectacle of the dull, dry, powdery mixtures being transformed by terrific heat into attractive, or sometimes unattractive, glazes seem overwhelming. Some teachers and potters also have a puritan attitude which insists that potters should develop their own glazes; such an argument ignores the fact that potters have been developing glazes for centuries and from them we learn a great deal and build upon their knowledge. What better starting point than a book of glaze recipes?

From recipes we can learn how materials behave, what effect the ingredients have on each other and on the various colouring oxides. By simple adjustments with the ingredients the glaze can be made either more shiny, more matt, more opaque; maturing temperatures can be lowered or made higher.

In this book the glazes are divided into sections according to the firing temperature required. Within each section the glazes are further divided into various groups according to how they appear when fired – that is in transparent, matt, opaque, coloured and other glaze groups, so that the potter can refer easily to the section required. Some glazes require such materials as wood ash and natural local clays, and where these are unobtainable similar substitutes must be made: the recipes here act as useful starting points, for potters must first test out their own materials and results will inevitably vary. However, such glazes often have rich decorative surfaces unobtainable by any other means. As such the recipes give the potter a well tried basic recipe with which to work.

There is also a large group of glazes which gives good results over a wide temperature range. With the increased awareness about dwindling fossil fuels and the ever rising cost of obtaining them, potters, along with other members of society, are very conscious of the need for energy conservation. Most potters prefer to fire stoneware temperature when the body becomes vitrified and stronger and the glaze effects more varied, but they also want to achieve these effects at as low a temperature as possible. For this reason, this wide firing range of glazes is of particular interest. At 1200°C (2192°F) most bodies are almost vitrified and all these glazes give good workable results. At higher temperatures the glaze changes, but sometimes not drastically so, and these glazes extend the glazer's range in many ways.

All potters' materials vary slightly from batch to batch, and from source to source. The suppliers take great care to provide materials with as consistent an analysis as possible, but even they cannot eliminate all the slight 'impurities' nature has introduced. For this reason it is sensible to test all recipes with your materials before large batches of glaze are made: if inconsistencies occur then a slight adjustment may be necessary. In the chapter on glaze preparation and adjustment, guidance is provided on how this can be done successfully.

All the recipes given in this book include descriptions of the glazes. Some are full and detailed, others are much shorter where no further explanation is necessary. But they are my own descriptions and may not match up to the glaze as it comes out in other firings. The earthenware glazes have been fired on both a red earthenware body and on a white firing earthenware body, the medium stoneware glazes on a red earthenware body, a medium stoneware body and on porcelain. All the stoneware glazes have been fired on a medium coloured stoneware body and on porcelain. Descriptions relate to these fired results. On lighter or darker coloured bodies colours and surface qualities vary. However precise the recipe and however careful the description and preparation, it is always necessary for each potter to test the glaze using his own glaze materials, clays and kilns before mixing up big batches.

The glaze materials

Almost all the materials used in this book have been ordered from pottery suppliers and are generally reliably obtainable though materials do vary from supplier to supplier and from batch to batch. Few potters are able or find it necessary to collect their own materials, though there are locally available materials (such as wood ash) which the potter does like to use. Glazes are made up of three different sorts of materials – fluxes which make the glaze melt, the amphoteric or stabilizing materials which give the glaze 'flesh', and acidic oxides which are the glass forming part or 'bone' of the glaze. With only a few exceptions, most glaze materials are mixtures and combinations of materials from each of these groups, and a check through the recipes will show that most glazes include them all. From the point of view of economy, the range of materials has been kept to a minimum, but many minerals do offer their own qualities, though substitutes can often be made.

All the glaze materials supplied by the pottery manufacturers are washed and finely ground. Some come as a fine powder (most have been passed through a 300 mesh sieve), some as lumps, but all are ready for use. Other materials like wood ash, granite or local clay need special preparation, and this is explained below, but other materials can be used as supplied. They should be stored in containers, clearly labelled with the name of the material as well as the date on which it was bought, and the name of the supplier.

Materials which come about naturally and can be collected and prepared by the potter have a fascination both for their cheapness and their unique qualities, yet it is these qualities which make them unreliable to quote in glaze recipes. For this reason tests are always essential. It is not possible here to describe all the variations and the different effects that can be obtained, but there are a few useful points about their preparation.

Wood ash

Wood ash is perhaps the most variable – and most useful. The sort of tree, shrub or plant, the soil in which it was grown, and even the time of year at which the plant was cut down are all factors which will affect the content of the ash. Ideally ash should be well burnt – either in a hearth or bonfire, and all the fine particles collected and carefully stored in a lidded container.

The ash can be used as an ordinary glaze ingredient in this unwashed state with the bits of carbon and unburnt wood still present. Most of these will be removed when the glaze is sieved, and this ash will make a much more speckled glaze. Alternatively the ash can be carefully prepared by washing and sieving beforehand by putting it carefully into a large bucket of water and stirring well. The unburnt wood and carbon will float to the top and the fine ash will slowly settle. After a few hours the water will dissolve the soluble salts of potassium and sodium and become a pale yellow colour; the water should be poured or syphoned off.

This procedure needs to be repeated three times if the ash is to be washed properly. This mixture, using plenty of water, should be passed through an 80 mesh sieve and allowed to settle. As much of the water should be removed as possible, and the ash sludge should be allowed to dry out; a good method is to place it inside a biscuit fired bowl. The dry ash should be stored inside a labelled lidded container. Mixed ash from bonfires or hearths is most common (and this is what has been used in these recipes), but occasionally it is possible to obtain 'single' ashes like oak, apple or privet, all of which give distinct qualities in the glaze.

Local clays

Local clays are prepared in much the same way. They should be dried out completely, broken up into small lumps and these dropped into plenty of hot water. When they have slaked down, the clay slip should be thoroughly mixed up and the mixture put through an 80 mesh sieve. When this has settled, which will be a slow process (about 2-3 days) depending on the fineness of the particles, the water should be removed and the slip put out to dry.

Most local clays, particularly those rich in iron (average 8%) make excellent glaze materials – Albany slip clay, found near Albany, New York, is a famous example. A good clay slip will melt on its own at around 1250°C (2282°F) to form a dark coloured (usually brown or black) shiny glaze and can be used in glaze recipes to excellent effect. Unfortunately few local clays have the necessary small particle size to melt so well. This can be remedied by grinding the dry clay in a pestle and mortar – a slow process. A better method, if the equipment is available, is to mill the clay in a ball mill for three to four hours, which makes the clay much more fusible. The Fremington clay used in these recipes was ball milled for four hours.

Rocks

Rocks, particularly granites or slates, are another cheap and often fascinating source. These are best collected from granite quarries where fine dust often lies around sawing machines. When collected this is often sufficiently fine to use as it is. Otherwise it requires grinding or ball milling. Different outcrops will of course vary in composition and each batch must be tested in the glaze to see if the result is that required.

Colouring glazes

Many potters when they have discovered a range of good workable glazes often prefer to experiment with them rather than keep trying out different glazes. For instance, a reliable shiny clear glaze can be easily opacified by the addition of tin oxide or zirconium silicate. Such a glaze can also be coloured by adding metal oxides, underglaze colour or glaze stain. This section describes how various effects and colours can be obtained. It is necessary to point out, however, that glaze colours are affected very much by different conditions and factors. In the first instance the colour depends on the body of the pot, and how much iron it contains. Accordingly this will either darken or brighten the glaze. On white firing and porcelain bodies, colours will generally be brighter. Some bodies 'suck in' the colour and glaze to leave a roughish surface, while others, particularly the highly vitrified bodies, will render these glazes smooth and even.

The glaze colour and quality are also affected by the firing atmosphere of the kiln, whether it is oxidized or reduced. These differences in effect are described in the recipe notes.

The temperature reached, the length of firing and the thickness of the glaze application are also important considerations which affect the final appearance of the glaze. It is, therefore, essential to test the glaze with your own materials, on your own clay, and in your own kiln, to find out exactly how it will respond to individual conditions.

White glazes

Tin oxide (SnO_2) will make most shiny glazes opaque, and an addition of 8%–12% will give an opaque, cool blue-white.

Zirconium silicate ($ZrSio_4$) ('Zircon'), which is a less refined form of zirconium oxide, is used as an opacifier; 6%–15% is required to give a neutral or cream white. Commercially available opacifiers, based on zirconium, such as 'Disperson' and 'Zircopax' are excellent.

Coloured glazes

Chromium oxide (Cr_2O_3) in most glazes gives an opaque green glaze with additions of 0.5%–2%. In some glazes crimson reds and pinks are obtained with the chrome-tin-pink combination.

Cobalt carbonate ($CoCO_3$) produces a smooth blue glaze varying from pink mauve (in a dolomite glaze), and vivid blue in an alkaline glaze to midnight blue in a feldspathic glaze; additions range from 0.5%–3%, and results are not affected strongly by reduction or oxidation atmospheres.

Cobalt oxide (CoO) gives colour similar to cobalt carbonate but is, weight for weight, more powerful. The oxide tends to be less evenly distributed in the glaze and can cause blue specks.

Copper carbonate ($CuCO_3$) produces colours which range from pink (in dolomite glazes) and red (in reduction atmospheres) to green (in lead glazes) or brilliant turquoise (in alkaline glazes). Amounts required in the glaze range from 0.5% (for copper reds in reduction) to 2% (for alkaline turquoise in oxidation) to 4% for strong greens (in lead glazes).

Copper oxide (CuO) is almost exactly the same as the carbonate but is, weight for weight, much more powerful. Note that both copper carbonate and copper oxide tend to encourage the release of lead in lead glazes during the glaze firing making the lead soluble in acid solutions. For this reason lead glazes, particularly those with copper addition, should not be used on the inside of vessels used for holding food and drink of any kind.

Iron oxide, black (FeO) and red (Fe_2O_3) The black iron oxide is, weight for weight, more powerful than the red, but in most glazes better results are achieved with the synthetic red iron oxide. Depending on the amount of oxide added to the glaze (1%–15%) and the firing atmosphere, the colour may range from pale blue green to brown black red in reduction, and range from pale honey to olive brown or black red in oxidation, in feldspathic glazes. In the dolomite glazes colour tends to be more muddy and muted. Iron oxide can act as flux, particularly at the higher temperatures, and may cause glazes to run. A substitution of weight for weight iron oxide and a flux will combat this, but often the quality of a black brown tenmoku glaze depends on it 'running' on the pot.

Manganese carbonate ($MnCO_3$) gives pink mauve colours in alkaline and dolomite glazes and browns in feldspathic glazes, using 1%–8%.

Manganese dioxide (MnO_2) gives results similar to the carbonate but is, weight for weight, more powerful.

Nickel oxide (NiO) gives colours ranging from ice blue (with zinc oxide glazes), yellow (with zinc oxide and titanium dioxide), pink and mauve (with barium carbonate and zinc oxide) to muted greens and greys in most ordinary glazes. Amounts added range from 1%–3%.

Rutile ($FeTiO_3$) (light, medium and dark), sometimes called rutile sand, is an ore containing titanium with iron oxide. It gives buff or brown colours in oxidation in glazes which can be mottled or crystalline, and it opacifies the glaze. In reduction rich blue grey colours can be achieved. Amounts added may be 2%–15%.

Titanium dioxide (TiO_2) gives glazes a matt creamy white colour in oxidation, and is often used in crystalline glazes. In reduction it gives a rich blue grey mottled effect; 2%–10% can be added.

Vanadium pentoxide (V_2O_5) gives colours ranging from yellow to brown and tends to break up the glaze, added in amounts of 3%–8%.

Yellow ochre (Fe_2O_3) is a natural form of iron oxide containing clay, and gives similar effects in the glaze.

Mixing the glaze

For the sake of safety it is best if all ingredients are stored in clearly labelled bins, buckets or jars with lids. This means that dust is controlled and half-empty packets or sacks of material do not issue clouds of their powdery contents when disturbed. Potters need always to bear in mind the toxicity of the glaze materials they use. Most are perfectly safe but some are poisonous if eaten or inhaled even in small quantities. For instance any form of lead, most metal oxides and barium carbonate should all be labelled 'poisonous'. Good housekeeping – wet washing of surfaces and tools, regular vacuum cleaning, smooth surfaces and so on – will also reduce or eliminate any possible hazard. Common sense, care and control in the handling and use of glaze materials as well as with other materials cannot be emphasized too strongly.

Glazes are made up by carefully mixing weighed ingredients into water, then passing the mixture through a fine sieve to break up the lumps to provide a thorough homogeneous mixture. For ease of mixing and comparing ingredients all the recipes total 100 parts: oxide additions are listed as percentage additions to the total. Depending on the amount of glaze that is required, the quantities can be interpreted as grams or ounces; 100 grams will produce enough glaze to fill a small glass jar or yoghurt pot, 1000 grams will be enough for a large bucket.

Scales need to be sufficiently large to hold good sized amounts of materials. Balance kitchen scales are more accurate than spring scales, especially for measuring small amounts. For weighing out quantities for test glazes a small accurate balance is required – chemical or photographic balances are ideal, though special balances, usually quite expensive in price, are marketed by the pottery manufacturers. But any accurate set of scales will suffice. Occasionally old fashioned confectionery scales can be purchased cheaply in second-hand or junk shops.

Plastic buckets or bowls are ideal for mixing and containing the glaze – they are light in weight, quiet in use and easy to clean. Sizes vary from small 'honey tubs' (often cheaply obtainable from confectioners) to a standard household bucket. For glazes required in large quantities small waste bins or plastic dustbins can be purchased from hardware stores. Quantities of glaze are important for they determine the way pots are to be glazed. For instance the workshop potter will probably prefer to dip the pots in glaze, so a good sized barrel with plenty of glaze is required. For the potter working on a small scale smaller amounts of glaze may seem more desirable, but this does limit the method of glaze application which can only be applied either by pouring the glaze or painting it on the pot. Glaze can also be sprayed but this does need specialist and expensive equipment. All these methods are discussed in the section on glaze application.

To mix the glaze weigh out the dry ingredients and gently add these to water. Tick off the amounts on the recipe when they are added to the water; this helps to eliminate mistakes while mixing. Hot water helps to break up the ingredients more quickly, which should be left in the water to 'slake' down. Lumps will disintegrate and within a few hours a thick uneven sludge will form in the bottom of the barrel. Mix this up with the liquid so that a thinnish watery mixture is formed. This mixture should now be put twice through an 80 mesh seive using a glaze brush or a domestic washing-up brush. This process will break up any tiny lumps and form a homogeneous, evenly mixed glaze. Ensure that as much glaze material passes through the seive as possible.

At this stage the glaze, too thin to use on pots, should be allowed to settle. To test this for glaze thickness, dip a finger or a piece of biscuited pot into the well stirred mixture. If the glaze runs off it is too thin. Allow the glaze to settle so that the ingredients sink to the bottom. Depending on the ingredients of the glaze this will take from one to twenty four hours. High clay glazes, for instance, are slower to settle, while materials high in non-plastic ingredients like frits will settle quickly.

Remove plenty of clear water from the top, either by carefully ladling it out or by syphoning it off with a rubber tube. Thoroughly mix up the glaze using either your hand or a large kitchen swish. Again test for thickness. For pouring or dipping the pot, the glaze should have the thickness of single cream. It should give the hand a good coating and as a general guide it should form a thickness of glaze on the pot which, when dry, can be scratched to leave a clean and identifiable mark.

Different glazes require different thicknesses; choice will depend on personal preference. Some glazes change in colour and texture when they are thicker and it is always worthwhile checking this with a single and a double thickness. Potters who want a more scientific test of glaze thickness can use a hydrometer, which measures the density (known as the specific gravity, SG) of the mixture. A simple instrument can be made by weighing a length of wood about 30cm (12in) long at one end. Drop this into the mixed glaze when it is at the consistency required and mark on the stick with waterproof paint the point where it goes into the glaze. On subsequent occasions if the glaze is too thin the mark will disappear below the surface; if it is too thick the mark will be above the surface.

An alternative method is to check the weight of the glaze. An empty glass jar with a volume of 1kg or 1lb is first weighed and then filled with glaze of the correct consistency and weighed again, then the original weight of the empty jar is subtracted. For an average glaze, for use on porous biscuit, 1500 grams to a litre (31½ ounces to a pint) is approximately correct. For glaze which is to be applied to a more vitrified body a higher density, about 1600 grams to a litre (34 ounces to a pint) is necessary. These weights are only approximate guides, for it is the prepared thickness which is important. Equally a glaze which is to be applied raw to unfired pots may have to be even thicker.

All glazes listed in this book have a quantity of a plastic material such as ball clay or bentonite in the recipe to help glaze suspension and to help bind the glaze when it is dry but not yet fired. This makes the glaze easier to handle as it is less likely to chip or dust off the surface. Some glazes, particularly those with large amounts of non-plastic materials like nepheline syenite or Cornish stone, settle in the glaze barrel very quickly and may form a hard layer which is difficult to break up. Such glazes will often be made easier to handle by the addition of a few drops of water in which either calcium chloride or sodium chloride has been mixed. Only small quantities are required. This mixture has the effect of 'thickening' the glaze, but add this very carefully as too much will turn the glaze into an unusable jelly-like consistency.

Glazes should be stored in lidded containers and of course should be clearly and properly labelled. Some potters make little 'button' glaze tests on round clay discs and tie these onto the bucket as a visual reminder of the glaze qualities. This is particularly useful for the experimental potter who is constantly involved in glaze tests.

Applying the glaze

All the glazes listed in this book have been used on porous biscuit fired clay first fired to low biscuit temperature 980°C (1796°F). Many glazes, particularly those with a high clay content, can be used on raw unfired clay. These glazes will be indicated as such. All the comments refer to glaze applied in normal thickness unless marked otherwise.

The majority of studio potters apply their glaze by dipping the pot into it. This is quick, efficient and, provided there is sufficient glaze and the pot is handled well, gives an even covering of glaze. Areas which are required to be glaze free, like flanges and galleries, lids, or foot rings, can be painted either with hot wax or a water-based wax emulsion which will resist the glaze. When the glaze slop is well stirred, which with highly plastic ingredients can be a relatively slow process, the mixture should be checked for thickness and adjusted accordingly.

To dip, the pot should be held firmly, either on the foot ring or on the rim and foot ring, depending on the size of the pot, and dipped into the glaze. Depending on the thickness of the walls (thin walled pots need to be dipped more quickly) the pot should be left in the glaze for about two to three seconds, and should be gently moved around while it is in the glaze. Lift it out holding it upside down to drain thoroughly. Make sure no trapped air pockets have caused 'blind' spots of glaze inside the pot; when the surface has lost its shine it can be gently handled and the pot put aside to dry. Dab on glaze where the fingers have left scar marks or tiny bald patches on the rim or any other place. Avoid touching the pot any more than is necessary until it is quite dry.

Thin walled pots, or pots which are to be glazed inside and outside with different glazes, should have glaze poured first on the inside. Leave this to dry for several hours so if the walls have become completely saturated they can dry out. Any runs or dribbles of glaze on the outside should be sponged, scratched or rubbed off. The outside can now be glazed either by dipping the inverted pot, kept horizontal, into the glaze, or the outside can be glazed by pouring. For large pots or when only a small amount of glaze is available, pouring is a useful method. Insides of containers can be swilled out rapidly with glaze and the excess poured out. Speed is important if an even layer is to be obtained.

Pouring glaze on the outside also has to be done fairly quickly. On small pots this is no problem; the pot should be held over a bowl and glaze poured liberally from a jug down the sides. Large pots need to be stood on glaze sticks over a bowl, and the glaze poured evenly round the pot. Aim for full flow effects to ensure the covering is regular.

After being glazed the pots must be prepared for the kiln and this varies according to the pot and temperature. Earthenware pots are often glazed all over — inside, outside and underneath — and stood on stilts, 'spurs' or triangular points in the kiln. These are removed with a swift tap after the firing, and the tiny glaze scars smoothed over with a carborundum stone. Because of the sharp and dangerous edges round the glaze scar it is essential that this is done.

Pots taken to a higher temperature, when the body becomes non-porous, are best fired by being stood directly on the kiln shelf. The shelf should first be dusted lightly with alumina hydrate to prevent the pot sticking to it and to enable the pot to move across the shelf as it contracts. At stoneware temperature most clay bodies soften slightly (and become pyroplastic) and if stood on stilts would distort. Furthermore most bodies become non-porous around 1200°C (2192°F) and so do not absorb water on non-glazed areas. Foot rings and the base of the pots need to be cleaned of glaze either by scratching off the glaze or sponging it off with water.

Glaze also needs to be removed from the bottom of the wall, though the amount to wipe off depends on the viscosity of the glaze. A stiff glaze needs to be cleaned off by about 3mm (⅛in) while a runny glaze needs a much greater distance. This is particularly necessary for shiny crystalline glazes which depend for their success on the glaze moving over the surface of the pot. Such glazes need special attention both in their application (correct thickness is vital) and in their placing in the kiln; in too hot a spot the glaze will run too much, too cool and no crystals will form. It is also a wise precaution to place pots with these sorts of glazes on a pad of clay or on a layer of alumina sand to catch any glaze runs.

Besides dipping and pouring, glaze can be applied by painting or spraying. Both methods have their advantages. Painted glaze, unless it is in very small areas, needs to be applied in several coats with a broad brush, each layer being allowed to dry before the next is applied. Gum arabic added to the glaze mixture will bind the layer onto the pot and enable this to be done. One of the main advantages of paint application is the small quantity of glaze required; the mixture can be applied to either biscuit fired, non-fired or even vitrified pots; a further advantage is that the layers can be built up so that if desired a thicker layer than usual can be applied than by pouring or dipping.

Spraying glaze, a method common in industry, also has special advantages. For instance, glaze can be applied to a vitrified surface and can be used to cover large areas quickly; the spray can also be used for graduations of colour. Also, only small amounts of glaze are necessary.

Suitable equipment is essential: a spray gun and compressor, and a spray booth with an extractor fan with an outside exhaust. The fine airborne glaze spray should not be breathed in, nor should the glaze be allowed to settle on working surfaces; ideally a water curtain should trap any glaze and the spray booth outlet should be well away from the workshop. Glaze to be sprayed needs to be sieved through a 120 mesh sieve so that the spray nozzle does not become blocked. Some glazes, particularly if they have colouring oxides in them, benefit from being ground in a pestle and mortar or, better still, milled for a couple of hours to ensure even distribution of colour and avoid 'specking'.

Pots which are vitrified should be heated first to enable the sprayed glaze to dry more quickly from the surface. To use the spray, place the pot in the spray booth on a banding wheel and with the gun held 30–45cm (12–18in) away, glaze the pot with short bursts directed evenly round the pot as the wheel is slowly rotated. Do not direct the spray in one spot or the glaze will run. Build up a normal thickness of glaze ensuring that all the surfaces underneath handles, inside ridges and so on are properly coated. Estimating the surface thickness is more difficult with sprayed glazes but it can be tested by scratching it with a pin.

Any thin or bald patches on dipped or poured pots can be touched up with glaze; a large, floppy, soft-bristled glaze mop will blob on the correct amount. It is necessary to put more on than first seems necessary as when it dries it halves in thickness and any surplus can be gently rubbed down with the finger. Any runs or dribbles on the glaze surface can also be lightly rubbed down to make an even coat. Where lids are fired in place on the pot check that touching surfaces are clean and free from glaze and that glaze has been cleaned back from the edge so that the problem of 'sticking-in', caused by the glaze running into the seating, will be avoided. A thin wash of alumina sand and china clay painted in the galley will prevent the surfaces sticking together, and can be rubbed off with a carborundum stone after firing.

Adjusting the glaze

No recipe is infallible. Materials, bodies, firing conditions and so on vary and give slightly different results. It is necessary to have as much information about a glaze recipe as possible so that, if necessary, adjustments can be made. All the glaze recipes in this book have been used as described and the results obtained are detailed. Listed here are many practical, reliable recipes which give smooth stable glazes; there are also recipes which are more spectacular in effect. These latter glazes depend for their success on more precise firing conditions, and simple adjustments to the glaze recipe can be made which will help to make them work for slightly different conditions. All the glazes can be modified, and general notes and suggestions for this are listed below.

Runny glaze

A glaze which runs freely and causes the pot to adhere to the kiln shelf has either been applied too thickly or fired too high or soaked too long at top temperature. The remedy is the opposite of all these causes. Alternatively the glaze must be 'stiffened', or made less viscous by the addition of equal parts of china clay and flint to the glaze recipe; a starting point would be 3%–5% by weight of each material. This may of course affect the appearance of the glaze, and is a factor which must be borne in mind especially for crystalline or special effect glazes, when a low alumina content is essential. In this case it may be more useful to reduce the thickness of the glaze and slightly lower the firing temperature. Pots with glazes which have run freely can be ground off at the bottom, then reglazed and refired to a lower temperature.

Dry pinholed glaze surface

When a glaze melts it goes through many changes depending on the type and the content of the glaze. Shiny glazes, high in fluxes, melt dramatically, and bubble before evening out to form a clear glass. In contrast glazes which are more matt and opaque are often high in china clay and flint, both of which stabilize the glaze. In these glazes the melting and maturing process takes place over a longer period and over a wider temperature range. Bubbles and so on are slower to clear. If the temperature has been too low or too rapidly reached such glazes may be dry with pinholes; here the remedy is simply a slightly higher temperature or a longer soak at top temperature. Some glazes, particularly those which respond to reducing conditions, develop rich surfaces only when fully reduced. An under-reducing firing can leave them fluxed but dull in colour and quality.

If the temperature cannot be raised, then the glaze may benefit from a slightly increased amount of flux (the material that makes the glaze melt). This may be done either by reducing slightly the amounts of china clay and flint or increasing the fluxes in the recipe, such as whiting or dolomite. Alternatively small amounts (3%–4%) of a secondary flux may be introduced, such as alkaline frit or calcium borate frit. Gerstley borate or colemanite may be substituted for the frit. In these quantities the glaze temperature is effectively lowered without the quality of the glaze being drastically affected. Glazes on pots which have not reached temperature can be fired again.

Bubbled and cratered glaze

As described earlier, glazes go through a complex series of changes and reactions which are not necessarily stopped when the temperature is reached, when the glaze is said to be matured: the surface may continue to even out and smooth over and, depending on the rate of cooling, crystals may form. However, if the temperature goes on rising then the ingredients continue to react much more violently and, just as for example when a sugar solution is overheated it boils and burns, so a glaze can boil and bubble. So violent is this process that part of the glaze is given off as vapour and the glaze will not settle down; the result is a rough glaze surface often displaying craters with jagged edges. Incidentally this sort of glaze surface must not be confused with crater glazes which are deliberately sought effects which have cratered surface but are smooth with no jagged edges.

Bubbled and cratered glaze surfaces can be avoided by firing to a lower temperature or having a shorter soak period. Alternatively additions of china clay and flint to the glaze will raise the maturing temperature. On pots where overfiring has occurred the surface can be rubbed over with a carborundum stone and a further layer of glaze can be applied by gently heating the pot first, and refiring.

Crazing

The balance of the glaze between the glaze layer and the body of the pot is crucial to a well fitting and strong glaze. During the firing the glaze slowly melts and 'bites' into the surface of the pot to form a 'layer of interaction' between the glaze and the clay. Depending on the glaze ingredients this layer is either indistinct (as for example in an ash glaze) or, in glassy glazes, the glaze and body are two fairly distinct layers. In this sort of glaze the expansion of the glaze and the body should be more or less equal if a well fitting glaze is to be achieved. If the glaze has a large proportion of high expansion fluxes, such as sodium and potassium, they cause the glaze to expand greatly while it is melted: as the glaze cools these fluxes cause it to contract, often more than the body of the pot. When this happens the glaze develops fine hair-like cracks over its surface which effectively spreads and stretches it over the pot. This is a particularly bad fault on earthenware pots which are not vitrified as the craze lines allow moisture to be absorbed through the surface, into the pot. On domestic pots it may also be unhygienic. The remedy here is to biscuit fire the pot to a higher temperature to make the pot less porous.

On stoneware pots crazing is not so important from the hygienic point of view, but it does make the pot physically less strong. The comparison here is with plywood, where two layers give strength to the other. If one layer cracks and breaks up the other layer is drastically weakened. On functional pots which are handled frequently, crazing is a weakness.

On pots which are more decorative, such an effect can be very attractive and is known as crackle. The Chinese potters were masters of this technique. Depending on the glaze and position in the kiln, various crackle effects could be achieved, from long slender lined crackles to tiny angular islands. Often finely ground colouring oxides or inks were rubbed into the surface to heighten the crackle effect. To connoisseurs the crackle was an important aspect of the pot.

When crazing is a problem, the glaze has to be 'stiffened' to stop it melting so freely. Either the high expansion alkaline fluxes have to be replaced by those of lower expansion such as magnesia or lithium or the amount of flint has to be increased. A practical suggestion is to add small amounts of talc (a mineral consisting of magnesium and flint) to the glaze.

Other remedies are to fire the glaze to a different temperature, either slightly lower or higher. Amounts of boron added to the glaze in the form of calcium borate or gerstley borate will also help to correct this.

Shivering, shelling or peeling

Glaze which flakes off the pot at the rims, on the edge of handles, or on raised decoration, is the opposite problem to crazing and is known as shivering, shelling or peeling. It occurs during the cooling period when the body contracts more than the glaze, putting it under slight compression which gives the pot great strength. For all practical purposes this is the 'ideal' situation. However, when this compression is too great the glaze is literally forced off the rims of the pot or edges of the handles as flakes or slivers of glaze. This may happen as the pot cools, as it is taken from the kiln or after a period of days or weeks. It is unsightly and it is dangerous, for the glaze silvers may fall into food. In severe cases the compression may literally cause the pot to split into several pieces.

The cure is basically the opposite of that suggested for crazing and is aimed at making the glaze contract more on cooling. This is achieved by substituting high expansion fluxes for those with lower expansion and reducing the amount of flint. In practice, the flint can be replaced by feldspar or by alkaline fluxes. I have found that lowering the firing temperature also helps to correct this maddening fault; particularly irritating in this respect are some glazes high in iron oxide.

Dunting, cracking or spiral cracking

Pots can crack in the glaze firing for two main reasons. The first reason, shivering, has already been dealt with. The second, commonly called dunting, occurs when a pot is cooled too quickly either by a cool draught of air or because the door of the kiln is opened too soon. It is rare in electric kilns and more common in flame burning kilns. The crack often takes the form of a spiral round the pot, usually picking out the weakest point such as where the wall is slightly thinner or where the base and sides join. Too great a compression of the glaze will also encourage this to happen.

Dunting, as opposed to other forms of cracking, can be recognized by the characteristic of the crack: if it is a clean split showing clear distinctions between body and glaze layer the crack has occurred after the glaze has matured. Cracks which were present before glazing and firing will show smoother edges where the matured glaze has healed over the edges.

Draughts of any sort must be avoided. Kilns should not be 'cracked' or opened until 200°C (392°F), and kiln doors not disturbed until 100°C (212°F). The top damper can safely be opened at 400°C (752°F), never earlier. Spy holes should remain firmly clammed up so no through draughts are created. A further precaution is to ensure that the pot is glazed on both the inside and the outside so compression on both sides of the wall is equal.

Crawling

Glaze which forms into rolls and lumps, leaving bare patches on the surface of the clay, known as crawling, has two basic causes – dust or shrinkage of the glaze. Some glazes, particularly those containing tin oxide, if applied too thickly or over a dusty surface will crawl up into large fat lumps. The remedy here is to ensure that the pots are dust free by wet sponging the surface.

Avoid blowing off the dust, unless in a dust extraction booth, as this should not be inhaled. If the glaze needs a thick application, a small percentage (3%) of bentonite can be added to the glaze mixture. This sort of crawling can also happen over painted or sprayed underglaze decoration which acts like dust under the glaze. In this case a small amount of glaze or gum arabic needs to be mixed into the underglaze powder to bind it onto the pot.

The second major cause is a glaze which is too high in plastic ingredients: during drying the glaze contracts and forms small craze lines which break up the surface. During the firing these glaze 'islands' do not melt to form an all-over covering but go into lumps: this usually happens on biscuit fired pots. Such glazes can usually be successfully applied raw, that is directly onto unfired or green ware; they can be adapted for use on biscuit fired work by substituting non-plastic clay such as calcined clay, either molochite (china clay) or calcite (ball clay), weight for weight for plastic clay. Gently rubbing the dry surface of the glaze with the finger to smooth over and fill-in any cracks can also help. Rapidly heating the glaze before it has dried out slowly will also cause 'islands' to form.

Bloating

Bubbles or lumps which occur in the body of the fired body of the pot, which when broken, show no evidence of foreign matter, are known as bloats. They usually only occur at high temperature, either because the body is overfired (in which case there are many smaller lumps) or when carbon is trapped in the body. Carbon from the remains of plants and rotting vegetation are present in all clay bodies, to a greater or lesser extent. During the biscuit or first firing, the carbon burns away as carbon dioxide or carbon monoxide from 500°C (932°F) to 900°C (1652°F). During this period the firing must be sufficiently slow and with enough oxygen present to allow complete combustion of the carbon to take place; this is a slower process on pots with thicker walls. If the firing is too rapid, the walls of the pot begin to vitrify and prevent the carbon gases from escaping or the heat does not soak through sufficiently; during the later glaze firing the trapped carbon turns into gas and expands and as the body softens causes a bloat or bubble to form; sometimes the surface is split.

The remedy here is to fire the body to a lower temperature or, more practically, slow down the speed of the biscuit firing. Many potters 'soak' their kiln at 900°C (1652°F) for one to two hours to enable all carbon to be burnt off. Some clays have a higher carbon content than others, and kilns can emit quite thick clouds of slightly blue and acrid tasting smoke. Ventilation to remove these gases is essential, as in too large quantities they are quite dangerous and a build up of the gas can occur slowly if sufficient precautions are not taken.

Quick-fire kilns

In recent years the so-called quick-fire kiln has come into widespread use. Lined with highly efficient insulating material, either in the form of a blanket fibre or 'solid' brick, the kilns have many advantages, not least of which is their ability to 'fast fire' – to reach temperature in a fraction of the time taken by the more traditional kilns lined with white firebricks. Kilns fired by flame-burning fuels, such as oil and gas, and by electricity have all come on to the market. They are lightweight, are smaller in size than conventional kilns in relationship to their packing space (because the insulating material need only be 5 or 7.5cm [2 or 3in] thick as opposed to 30cm [12in]), they are cheaper to build (no heavy framework is required) and, most importantly, because they are more efficient at retaining heat they cost much less to fire.

While such kilns have enormous advantages they also pose problems for the studio potter. All the glazes in this book have been fired in conventional kilns with 'solid' walls. They are comparatively slow to reach top temperature and just as slow to cool down. All the stoneware firings, for example, took approximately 10–12 hours to reach temperature, while the earthenware firing took 6–8 hours. The final 100°C (180°F) of temperature is reached over a period of about 2 hours with stoneware glazes fired in the electric kiln. While firing at such a slow speed no soak is required at top temperature. With earthenware glazes (all of which were fired in the electric kiln) a soak of approximately 20–30 minutes was maintained at top temperature.

Glazes fired in the reduction kiln, for glazes in this book (a 12 cu. ft natural gas kiln) were reduced from 1050°C (1922°F) until 1260°C (2300°F). Alternate periods of oxidation and reduction (roughly every 20 minutes) were followed to enable the temperature to rise. (In this kiln reduction tended to hold temperature rather than allow it to rise.) At 1260°C (2300°F) a period of about 20 minutes' oxidation was introduced to clear the atmosphere and ensure an even heat. The time and temperatures of each firing should be recorded.

When using fast-fire kilns, to obtain similar results with the glazes a similar firing schedule must be followed. To enable the kiln to go up in temperature more slowly, it needs to be fitted with suitable controlling devices. The electric kiln, for example, needs either an input regulator, such as a 'Sunvic', or a 'Simmerstat'. The 'Sunvic' has a dial which indicates from 0–100. When set at 0 there is zero input – the kiln is off; at 100 the kiln is fully on. Graduations on the scale in between are proportional, i.e. when set at 50 the kiln elements are on for a period (usually about 50 seconds) then off for the same period. An alternative is the 'Simmerstat' which has settings for 'off', 'low', 'medium', 'high', 'full'. The aim of using the controls is to allow the temperature to build up slowly. The attraction of these fast-fire kilns is that, by manually adjusting the switches, a much lower input of power is used to reach temperature, and therefore they are much less costly to fire than similar sized conventional kilns.

Gas and oil fired kilns are less easily controlled than electric kilns. The manufacturers of these kilns usually supply detailed information on how to make the best use of the burners etc., but the basic aim, of limiting fuel input to slow down temperature rise, remains the same. The difficulty is that many burners will not operate safely on 'low' settings: the flame may blow out or not remain lit at all. However, with most sophisticated and sensitive control mechanisms these problems are being overcome, and more controlled firings are possible.

A firing is not complete until top temperature has been reached and the kiln is cooled. Glazes, as is explained elsewhere in the book (p. 12), go through complex changes: melts occur, glass is formed and various minerals go into solution. At top temperatures the glaze evens out and smooths down. As the glaze cools, other changes occur. If the glaze is cooled rapidly, chemicals in solution stay there to give smooth clear glazes. If the glaze cools slowly, these materials begin to form crystals and opaque or matt surfaces result. If the temperature is held on cooling then large crystal formations will occur if suitable mixtures have been devised. For these reasons the rate at which the glaze cools helps determine the final result. Fast-fire kilns are also 'fast cool' and often the bright shiny surfaces of glazes may be due to too rapid cooling. If this occurs the kiln controls may need to be turned down to a low setting rather than to 'off' when top temperature is reached. This will slow the rate of cooling, particularly in the first 100°C (180°F). Ensure also that all spy-holes, dampers and flue controls are well sealed to prevent any through flow of air.

Glazes mature through a process of heat work rather than temperature achieved. In other words, the materials react and respond to each other slowly, and need time to achieve this. Equally, the reaction between the glaze and the body of the pot, often an important factor in introducing iron speckle into the glaze or enabling the glaze to break on the edges of rims and handles, needs a certain time to happen. For this reason there is often little virtue in speed of firing for its own sake. The final result of the fired glaze is what is required. The more efficiently and cheaply this can be achieved without loss of quality or interest in the glaze, the more one will appreciate the benefits of fast-fire kilns.

Clay slips

Clay slips applied to the unfired pot and used under glazes can serve two major purposes. They can be used to mask the surface of the pot with an inert layer which effectively separates the pot from the glaze, or they can be used to introduce a reactive layer, which in conjunction with the glaze gives a range of coloured textural, often decorative, effects which cannot be achieved by any other means.

Inert layers of slip are particularly useful if, for example, the body of the pot is of dark clay and a light coloured glaze is to be applied. The white slip recipe given on p. 21, and used as a base for the slip recipes in this book, does this very well. This sort of slip can be used to carry various colours, either in the form of metal oxides and/or commercially produced glaze or body stains. Generally speaking, glaze stains have more colouring pigment weight for weight than body stains and are more finely ground. Consequently they are considerably more expensive to buy. Some coloured slips (such as the green slip listed here) will be inert under some glazes, and 'reactive' with others. 'Reactive' slips respond to the fluxing action of the glaze and break through the glaze layer giving mottled or broken textures. Often such slips are loaded with colouring oxides which can act as a flux, or they are an 'imbalance', with an excess of one material. A high silica content in the slips, for example, will encourage a glaze/slip reaction which can give extraordinarily interesting results. The process of linking glaze and slip into one unified whole is well established, both within the ceramic industry and to studio potters, but there is scant information on it. The use of slips here is only a small part of the repertoire the enthusiastic potter can enjoy.

Like all recipes, success depends not only on having the correct ingredients (which always vary from batch to batch) but on having the 'right' thickness of slip and of glaze. This depends on the porosity of the clay and the biscuit fired pot, and on the thickness of the slip and clay mixture. The results described in this book were obtained by a systematic method. This involved slip which had the consistency of single cream into which the pot, when it was bone dry, was dipped. When the shine had left this layer (which usually took less than a minute) it was partly dipped again so that a double layer was obtained. After biscuit firing to 980°C (1796°F) the glaze was applied. Again the pots were dipped into this, and the consistency was about that between milk and single cream. Clays which are porous at this temperature (a good example is porcelain) will tend to absorb more glaze than those (such as an earthenware clay) which are harder. Again, therefore, some discretion is needed in deciding what is a 'reasonable' thickness. Most glazes require a thickness of between 1.5–3mm ($\frac{1}{16}$–$\frac{1}{8}$in). Usually a thick layer of slip will 'burn' through a thin layer of glaze, and, as for example in iron slips, saturate it with colour. This may be the desired result, but with a much thicker application of glaze the effect is more likely to be mottled and broken.

Generally, the more the slip is 'fluxed', as for example with metal oxides (a useful instance is a 'black' slip for earthenware glazes, made up of red ball clay 100% plus iron oxide 6, manganese dioxide 4, cobalt oxide 2) most transparent glazes will fire black, but under opaque glazes it will 'break through' to give black and blue mottled effects. In this combination the slip is fluxing through the stiffer glaze and similar effects are achieved with the slips given here, but it should be noted that the use of slip under the glaze introduces another variable element in the glaze, and results may not always be as expected. Consistency of results requires careful applications of slip and glaze at the correct consistency.

The slips

The glazes which yielded interesting results are detailed after the appropriate glaze by the use of reference initials (i.e. BS for blue slip). The slip with a thickness of single cream was applied by dipping on to the leather dry clay. This was biscuit fired before being dipped again in the glaze.

The slip recipes

Rutile slip (RS)

Red clay	30
Ball clay	50
Flint	20
+ Rutile	25

Iron slip (IS)

Ball clay	51
Flint	40
+ Crocus martis	9

Green slip (GS)

Red clay	40
Ball clay	40
Flint	20
+ Copper carbonate	2.25
Chrome oxide	1

Blue slip (BS)

Red clay	80
Flint	20
+ Cobalt oxide	1.5
Nickel oxide	1

White slip (WS)

Borax frit	15
Nepheline syenite	30
Ball clay	30
China clay	15
+ Disperson	10

Yellow slip (YS)

Nepheline syenite	19
Feldspar	52
Yellow ochre	19
Ball clay	10
+ Crocus martis	8

Glaze temperature and classification

There are many different ways of classifying glazes – according to the ingredients, the colour, the opacity of the glaze or even the use to which the glaze will be put. The most common method and perhaps the clearest and most easily understood is to divide up the glazes according to the temperature at which they mature, which is the method I have used here. Glazes fall into three main groups – low temperature 1000°C–1150°C (1832°F–2102°F) for earthenware, medium temperature 1200°C–1220°C (2192°F–2228°F) for stoneware, and high temperature 1250°C–1280°C (2282°F–2336°F) for stoneware and porcelain. Within these categories the glazes have been further arranged under a total of eight sections. Most glazes can successfully be coloured or stained by additions of metal colouring oxides: where this has resulted in attractive effects this will also be mentioned and many of the possibilities listed, but not all the recipes have been tested with every variation of colouring oxide, and potters could experiment with prepared glazes for other effects.

Within each section, glazes are divided under sub-headings starting with transparent and semi-transparent, opaque and matt, coloured glazes, and base and decorative glazes.

Health and safety

No materials used by the potter should ever be inhaled or ingested, for all are to some extent harmful. The actual degree of toxicity depends on the particular material, how finely it has been ground and the amount taken into the body. Some are more poisonous than others; for example, nickel oxide, zinc oxide, copper oxide, copper carbonate, chromium oxide, barium carbonate, flint and lead bisilicate all require special care in handling, but with a commonsense approach danger can be avoided. Good housekeeping will deal with the problems.

(1) Keep all materials in properly labelled bins, jars or holders with well-fitting lids.
(2) When mixing glazes always add glaze materials to water, gently letting them slide into the water; avoid dropping them and so creating dust.
(3) Work in a well ventilated room.
(4) Wipe up any spilled glaze material or splashed glaze with a damp cloth. Wash off all utensils before they dry out to avoid dust contamination.
(5) Scrub hands, particularly nails, after mixing and handling glaze.
(6) Do not eat or drink while mixing glazes.

Lead

The superiority of lead glazes for the earthenware potter lies in their brilliance, lustre and smoothness; unfortunately lead is a poisonous material and most countries have special regulations governing its use. Most potters are now aware of the dangers in the use of lead. As a raw material it is a poison which, if taken into the body through the mouth, the lungs, or absorbed through cuts or scratches, builds up in the body and is difficult to break down and release. For this reason the raw forms of lead are avoided in the workshop and lead frits are used instead. Lead bisilicate is the safest form.

In a fired glaze lead can be soluble even in weak acid solutions where there is an imbalance in the construction of the glaze. For this reason it is best to avoid lead glazes on vessels intended to store or serve food or drink, unless they have first been tested for lead solubility at an established and reputable laboratory.

The glaze recipes

All the recipes are listed as parts by weight, and amounts are expressed as percentages. All the glaze ingredients are listed with the fluxes first then the clays and finally the flint. Additions to the basic glaze recipes are expressed as percentage parts by weight over and above the basic glaze; such materials are listed at the bottom of the recipe.

All of the materials are easily obtained from pottery suppliers (except for local materials) but variations do occur and batches should be tested first. Where feldspar is included in the recipe, this refers to potash feldspar. Where soda feldspar is required, this is specifically mentioned. Feldspars in the United States often have names or numbers, and direct substitutions can be made according to type. The list of materials at the end of the book gives the full range of equivalents available in the USA. Where materials are included in brackets in the recipes, this is to indicate close American equivalents.

1060°–1080°C (1940°–1976°F) Orton cone 04

1. Transparent, white and opaque glazes

1 Bright transparent

Lead bisilicate	85
Zinc oxide	5
China clay	10

A bright transparent glaze.

2 Clear transparent

Calcium borate frit (P2954) (Colemanite)	40
Zinc oxide	5
Whiting	20
Soda feldspar	15
Quartz	6
China clay	14

A smooth bright transparent glaze. 1060°C (1940°F)

3 A clear transparent glaze

Lead bisilicate	80
China clay	20

A slightly frosty glaze at 1080°C (1976°F) with a pale creamy white hue.

4 A clear glaze

Calcium borate frit (P2954) (Colemanite)	55
Nepheline syenite	10
Flint	5
China clay	30

A smooth clear glaze. 1060°C (1940°F)

5 Transparent

Calcium borate frit (P2954) (Colemanite)	50
Soda feldspar	35
Ball clay	10
Flint	5

A smooth transparent glaze. 1060°C (1940°F)

6 A clear glaze

Lead bisilicate	70
Feldspar	20
Zinc oxide	2
Whiting	3
China clay	5

A clear, slightly crazed glaze. 1060°C (1940°F)

7 Clear transparent

Borax frit (P2957)	33
Lead bisilicate	40
Whiting	5
Feldspar	10
Zinc oxide	9
Bentonite	3

A smooth clear transparent glaze; will craze if applied too thickly. 1060°C (1940°F)

8 Clear lead glaze

Lead bisilicate	90
China clay	10

A clear useful lead glaze.

Additions

(*a*) With iron oxide 14%, adventurine effect results at higher temperatures. Below 1100°C (2012°F) the colour is dull.

(*b*) With chromium oxide 0.75%, a holly green glaze results.

9 Transparent lead glaze

Lead bisilicate	70
Whiting	7
Feldspar	13
China clay	10

A smooth bright transparent glaze. 1060° (1940°F)

10 Soft milky white

Lead bisilicate	70
Feldspar	20
Zinc oxide	5
China clay	5
+ Tin oxide	5

A semi-opaque, soft milky white glaze. 1080°C (1976°F)

11 A milky clear glaze

Calcium borate frit (P2954) (Colemanite)	60
Feldspar	25
Flint	5
China clay	10

A milky clear glaze, opaque where thick. 1060°C (1940°F)

12 Frosty clear

Lead bisilicate	70
Soda feldspar	30

A frosty clear glaze at 1080°C (1976°F); runny at 1150°C (2093°F)

13 Frosty clear

Calcium borate frit (P2954) (Colemanite)	45
Whiting	4
Soda feldspar	47
China clay	4

A clear, slightly crazed glaze. 1060°C (1940°F)

14 Bright clear glaze

Calcium borate frit (P2954) (Colemanite)	50
Feldspar	35
Barium carbonate	12
Bentonite	3

A clear bright well-fitting glaze on the white body; an opalescent, milky effect on the red earthenware. 1060°C (1940°F)

15 Clear bright lead glaze

Lead bisilicate	79
Whiting	6
China clay	15

A smooth clear well-fitting transparent glaze. 1060°C (1940°F)

16 Soft, semi-transparent

Lead bisilicate	60
Borax frit (P2957)	18
Feldspar	10
China clay	10
Flint	2
+ Zircon	10

A soft semi-transparent glaze, less opaque on red-coloured bodies.

17 Blue white

Calcium borate frit (P2954) (Colemanite)	80
Flint	10
China clay	10
+ Zirconium oxide	10

A blue white, semi-opaque glaze over white body, less opaque over red clay. 1080°C (1976°F)

18 Silky smooth white

Lithium carbonate	12
Barium carbonate	5
Whiting	12
Zinc oxide	12
China clay	20
Flint	39

A silky smooth white glaze over white body (not over red). 1060°C (1940°F)

Addition

(*a*) With copper carbonate 2%, a silky mottled attractive mid-green develops.

19 Creamy white

Lead bisilicate	80
Flint	8
Zircon	12
+ Bentonite	4

A creamy white glaze, richer on light-coloured clays.

20 Silky semi-matt

Lead bisilicate	45
Whiting	10
Zinc oxide	5
Feldspar	25
China clay	15

A smooth silky semi-matt glaze.

21 Semi-matt vellum glaze

Lead bisilicate	65
Feldspar	7
Zinc oxide	15
China clay	13

A pale creamy white vellum-type matt glaze. 1060°C (1940°F)

22 Matt

Alkaline frit (P2962)	65
Whiting	10
Cornish (Cornwall) stone	15
China clay	10

A semi-opaque matt glaze at 1060°C (1940°F) with an attractive crackle.

23 Matt smooth glaze

Alkaline frit (P2962)	15
Lead bisilicate	40
Whiting	5
Zinc oxide	5
Feldspar	20
China clay	15

A smooth matt glaze for decorative surfaces. 1080°–1100°C (1976°–2012°F)

2. Coloured glazes

24 Rich turquoise green

Calcium borate frit (P2954) (Colemanite)	46
Whiting	4
Soda feldspar	45
China clay	5
+ Copper oxide	3

A rich turquoise green over a white body or slip. 1060°C (1940°F)

25 Matt turquoise blue

Soda feldspar	48
Calcium borate frit (P2954) (Colemanite)	10
Barium carbonate	12
Zinc oxide	4
Whiting	12
Flint	10
Ball clay	4
+ Copper carbonate	1.5

A matt turquoise blue at 1080°C (1976°F), more shiny at higher temperatures.

26 Bright pea green

Lead bisilicate	93
China clay	7
+ Tin oxide	5
Chrome oxide	0.25

A bright shiny pea green-coloured, semi-opaque glaze on white and red bodies. 1060°C (1940°F)

27 Transparent holly green

Lead bisilicate	91
China clay	4
Bentonite	3
Flint	2
+ Chrome oxide	0.5

A bright holly green transparent glaze.

28 Matt antique green

Lead bisilicate	55
Whiting	12
Feldspar	23
China clay	8
Flint	2
+ Cobalt carbonate	0.5
Iron oxide	6

A matt antique green glaze.

29 Gun metal green

Lead bisilicate	83
Feldspar	13
Bentonite	4
+ Rutile	7
Cobalt carbonate	1

A smooth gun-metal green glaze. 1060°–1100°C (1940°–2012°F)

30 Smooth opaque green

Lead bisilicate	90
Whiting	2
China clay	5
Feldspar	3
+ Tin oxide	8
Chrome oxide	0.75

A smooth opaque bright holly green. 1080°C (1976°F)

31 Deep ink blue

Calcium borate frit (P2954) (Colemanite)	43
Whiting	4
Soda feldspar	45
China clay	8
+ Cobalt oxide	1
Iron oxide	1

A rich deep inky blue. 1060°C (1940°F)

32 Dark transparent blue

Lead bisilicate	80
Borax frit (P2957)	13
China clay	7
+ Copper carbonate	1
Cobalt carbonate	1

A dark transparent blue glaze on light-coloured bodies. 1060°C (1940°F)

33 Wedgwood blue

Lead bisilicate	56
Feldspar	10
Borax frit (P2957)	20
China clay	14
+ Zircon	10
Cobalt carbonate	3

An opaque semi-matt Wedgwood blue glaze.

34 Rich dark blue

Lead bisilicate	93
Flint	3
Bentonite	4
+ Zircon	8
Copper carbonate	2
Cobalt carbonate	2

A smooth rich dark blue glaze. 1080°C (1976°F)

35 Transparent red brown

Calcium borate frit (P2954) (Colemanite)	16
Lead bisilicate	40
Alkaline frit (P2962)	25
Zinc oxide	5
Nepheline syenite	5
China clay	9
+ Manganese dioxide	5

A smooth bright transparent red brown glaze over light-coloured bodies. Do not overfire. 1080°C (1976°F)

36 Orange brown

Lead bisilicate	77
Whiting	10
China clay	10
Zinc oxide	3
+ Zircopax	15
Iron Oxide	7

A bright orange brown glaze. 1080°C (1976°F)

37 Rich Rochester brown

Lead bisilicate	70
Whiting	3
Feldspar	15
Zinc oxide	5
China clay	4
Flint	3
+ Iron oxide	5
Manganese dioxide	5

A smooth rich black glaze; darker on red body. 1060°C (1940°F)

38 Rich Rockingham black

Lead bisilicate	83
Feldspar	10
China clay	7
+ Manganese carbonate	4
Iron oxide	4

A rich Rockingham black brown glaze; the high gloss adds to the attractive qualities of the glaze. 1080°C (1976°F)

39 Metallic black glaze

Lead bisilicate	80
Feldspar	14
China clay	6
+ Manganese carbonate	9
Iron oxide	3
Rutile	2

A smooth metallic black glaze. 1080°C (1976°F)

40 Black, mirror glossy glaze

Lead bisilicate	75
Whiting	6
China clay	9
Flint	10
+ Cobalt oxide	3
Iron oxide	2
Manganese carbonate	2

A bright black, mirror-like glossy glaze. 1080°C (1976°F)

41 Matt black

Lead bisilicate	80
Whiting	6
China clay	14
+ Cobalt carbonate	2
Iron oxide	2
Manganese carbonate	3

A matt black glaze. 1060°C (1940°F)

42 Lustrous black

Lead bisilicate	80
Whiting	2
Feldspar	10
Zinc oxide	3
China clay	5
+ Manganese dioxide	8

A lustrous deep black glaze, smooth and rich. 1060°C (1940°F)

43 A bright lustrous black glaze

Lead bisilicate	75
Cornish (Cornwall) stone	22
Bentonite	3
+ Cobalt carbonate	1.5
Manganese carbonate	9

A bright lustrous black glaze with a mirror-like surface. 1060°C (1940°F)

44 Rich black

Lead bisilicate	78
Borax frit (P2957)	12
China clay	10
+ Manganese carbonate	9

A lustrous rich black glaze.

45 Clear glaze base

Borax frit (P2957)	65
Lead bisilicate	25
China clay	10

A bright clear glaze base. 1080°C (1976°F)

Additions

(*a*) With iron oxide 4% and manganese carbonate 4%, a rich mahogany brown.

(*b*) With chrome oxide 0.5%, a bright yellow over white body or slip.

(*c*) With cobalt carbonate 0.5% and manganese carbonate 2%, a rich purple results.

3. Decorative glazes

46 Rich clear Persian blue

Alkaline frit (P2962)	70
Flint	12
China clay	18
+ Copper carbonate	2

A bright clear Persian turquoise blue on white body. This high alkaline glaze does crackle and is difficult to handle, but the colour is superb. 1060°C (1940°F)

47 Alkaline clear base glaze

Alkaline frit (P2962)	75
Calcium borate frit (P2954) (Colemanite)	15
China clay	10

A runny base glaze which is best used on flat surfaces to give good colour response on white body. 1060°C (1940°F)

Additions

(*a*) With copper carbonate 2%, a transparent turquoise.

(*b*) With cobalt carbonate 0.5% and chrome oxide 0.5%, deep midnight blue.

(*c*) With copper oxide 2% and red iron oxide 1%, a green turquoise glaze results.

48 High alkaline glaze

Lead bisilicate	25
Alkaline frit (P2962)	70
Whiting	3
Bentonite	2

An alkaline base glaze for good colour response for manganese dioxide (purple mauves) and copper carbonate (turquoise) but suitable only for flat decorative surfaces. 1060°C (1940°F)

49 Egyptian turquoise

Alkaline frit (P2962)	57
Soda feldspar	28
Whiting	15
+ Copper oxide	4

A rich dark Egyptian turquoise-coloured matt glaze. 1080°C (1976°F)

50 Lava-textured green glaze

Lead bisilicate	55
Whiting	5
Feldspar	30
China clay	5
Flint	5
+ Chrome oxide	0.5
Vanadium pentoxide	5
Cobalt carbonate	0.5

A lava-textured bright green glaze. 1080°C (1976°F)

51 A mottled red green glaze

Calcium borate frit (P2954) (Colemanite)	10
Borax frit (P2957)	15
Alkaline frit (P2962)	10
Zinc oxide	3
Lead bisilicate	35
China clay	20
Flint	7
+ Tin oxide	1
Copper carbonate	0.5
Silicon carbide	0.5

A mottled local reduction copper red glaze. Good reds will develop on light-coloured body. 1060°–1100°C (1940°–2012°F)

52 Crystalline glaze

Lead bisilicate	51
Borax frit (P2957)	31
China clay	6
Rutile (light)	6
Zinc oxide	6

A smooth ochre yellow glaze which at higher temperatures develops creamy white crystals. 1060°–1100°C (1940°–2012°F)

Addition

(*a*) With copper carbonate 2.5%, cobalt carbonate 1%, a mid-sea green glaze develops.

1060°–1080°C (1940°–1976°F)

53 Bright black glaze

Lead bisilicate	80
Feldspar	12
China clay	8
+ Manganese carbonate	7
Iron oxide	4

A shiny bright black glaze. 1060°–1100°C (1940°–2012°F)

1060–1150°C (1940°–2093°F) Orton cones 04–01

1. Clear, opaque and white glazes

54 A clear glaze

Lead bisilicate	40
Borax frit (P2957)	40
China clay	20

A clear stable glaze.

55 A clear glaze

Lead bisilicate	70
Cornish (Cornwall) stone	20
China clay	10

A clear glaze at 1080°C (1976°F); a crystalline transparent at 1150°C (2093°F)

56 Transparent lead glaze

Lead bisilicate	60
Whiting	10
Feldspar	20
China clay	10

A semi-transparent glaze at below 1100°C (2012°F); clear around 1120°C (2048°F)

57 Clear glaze

Lead bisilicate	40
Borax frit (P2957)	30
Cornish (Cornwall) stone	20
China clay	10

A slightly milky glaze at 1080°C (1976°F); clear and stable at 1150°C (2093°F)

58 Frosty clear

Alkaline frit (P2962)	65
Zinc oxide	10
Cornish (Cornwall) stone	15
China clay	10

A frosty transparent glaze at 1080°C (1976°F); a clear glaze at 1150°C (2093°F)

59 Transparent

Alkaline frit (P2962)	35
Feldspar	10
Whiting	10
China clay	30
Flint	15

A transparent slightly matt glaze. 1100°C (2012°F)

60 Clear stiff transparent

Lead bisilicate	60
Feldspar	30
Whiting	5
China clay	5

A clear stiff transparent glaze. 1080°–1100°C (1976°–2012°F)

61 Clear glaze

Lead bisilicate	65
Feldspar	10
Whiting	5
Zinc oxide	5
China clay	10
Flint	5

A clear glaze which tends to craze. 1080°–1150°C (1976°–2093°F)

62 Clear

Alkaline frit (P2962)	15
Lead bisilicate	35
Feldspar	30
Whiting	5
Flint	10
China clay	5

A smooth clear glaze. 1150°C (2093°F)

63 A clear glaze

Cornish (Cornwall) stone	20
Lead bisilicate	75
Bentonite	5

A clear bright glaze. 1080°–1150°C (1976°–2093°F)

64 Smooth clear

Alkaline frit (P2962)	30
Lead bisilicate	35
Soda feldspar	5
Whiting	7
China clay	10
Flint	13

A smooth clear glaze. 1080°–1150°C (1976°–2093°F)

65 Clear milky glaze

Borax frit (P2957)	85
Ball clay	15

A stable clear slightly milky glaze at 1060°C (1940°F); transparent at 1150°C (2093°F)

66 Stiff semi-transparent

Lead bisilicate	85
Barium carbonate	3
China clay	12

A creamy stiff semi-transparent glaze. 1080°–1150°C (1976°–2093°F)

67 Semi-transparent cream

Lead bisilicate	65
Feldspar	10
Talc	6
China clay	5
Flint	14

A semi-transparent yellow cream glaze at 1080°C (1976°F); more clear at 1150°C (2093°F)

68 Smooth semi-matt

Lead bisilicate	20
Borax frit (P2957)	40
Whiting	13
Feldspar	17
Quartz	5
China clay	5

A smooth semi-matt glaze at 1080°C (1976°F); more transparent at higher temperatures 1150°C (2093°F)

69 Semi-matt

Lead bisilicate	70
Feldspar	15
Barium carbonate	7
Bentonite	8

A semi-matt glaze at 1060°C (1940°F); a clear glaze at 1150°C (2093°F)

70 Smooth semi-clear

Lead bisilicate	66
Cornish (Cornwall) stone	15
Whiting	5
China clay	14

A smooth semi-clear glaze.

71 Soft opaque white

Lead bisilicate	45
Borax frit (P2957)	23
Zinc oxide	7
China clay	15
Flint	10
+ Tin oxide	6

A smooth opaque glaze at 1080°C (1976°F); rich iron red white over red clay at higher temperatures, 1150°C (2093°F)

72 White opaque

Feldspar	30
Calcium borate frit (P2954) (Colemanite)	30
Zinc oxide	5
Barium carbonate	4
Whiting	2
Flint	24
China clay	5

A white opaque glaze at 1080°C (1976°F). At higher temperatures, 1150°C (2093°F), pale blue opalescent effects develop, especially pronounced on red body.

73 Opaque white

Borax frit (P2957)	68
Zinc oxide	12
China clay	20
+ Tin oxide	8

A smooth opaque matt white. 1150°C (2093°F)

1060°–1150°C (1940°–2093°F)

74 A creamy opaque

Lead bisilicate	50
Borax frit (P2957)	31
Zinc oxide	8
Titanium dioxide	6
China clay	5

A creamy opaque glaze which will give crystalline effects. 1080°–1150°C (1976°–2093°F)

75 Vellum matt cream

Lead bisilicate	56
Borax frit (P2957)	24
Zinc oxide	8
China clay	8
Titanium dioxide	4
+ Zirconium silicate	8
Tin oxide	4

A smooth vellum matt opaque at 1080°C (1976°F); brighter at 1150°C (2093°F)

76 Smooth vellum

Lead bisilicate	50
Whiting	10
Feldspar	20
China clay	15
Flint	5

A smooth semi-opaque creamy vellum glaze at 1080°C (1976°F); more transparent at 1150°C (2093°F)

77 Milky white

Lead bisilicate	10
Alkaline frit (P2962)	55
Feldspar	20
China clay	15
+ Zirconium silicate	12

A milky white opaque glaze at 1080°C (1976°F); at 1150°C (2093°F) a shiny mottled white over red body.

78 Cream matt

Lead bisilicate	60
China clay	25
Whiting	5
Zinc oxide	10
+ Rutile	4

A cream matt glaze. 1080°–1100°C (1976°–2012°F)

1060°–1150°C (1940°–2093°F)

2. Coloured glazes

79 Rich honey

Lead bisilicate	44
Feldspar	30
Whiting	5
Zinc oxide	6
Flint	5
China clay	10
+ Iron oxide	2

A rich honey-coloured glaze, brighter at higher temperatures. 1080°–1150°C (1976°–2093°F)

80 A soft turquoise

Alkaline frit (P2962)	47
Whiting	15
Feldspar	28
Flint	10
+ Zircon	30
Copper oxide	2

A soft turquoise-coloured glaze. 1150°C (2093°F)

81 Brown transparent glaze

Lead bisilicate	50
Whiting	10
Feldspar	20
China clay	8
Flint	12
+ Iron oxide	8

A rich yellow brown transparent glaze. 1150°C (2093°F)

82 Opalescent white

Lead bisilicate	75
Nepheline syenite	20
China clay	5
+ Tin oxide	6

A milky opalescent white, attractive iron red mottle over red clay. 1150°C (2093°F)

83 Crimson red

Lead bisilicate	75
Feldspar	5
Flint	18
Bentonite	2
+ Tin oxide	6
Iron oxide	5

A crimson red glaze on white body. 1100°–1150°C (2012°–2093°F)

1060°–1150°C (1940°–2093°F)

84 Viridian green

Calcium borate frit (P2954) (Colemanite)	35
Zinc oxide	5
Soda feldspar	35
Quartz	10
China clay	15
+ Copper oxide	3

A rich viridian green glaze, brighter over a white body or slip. 1080°–1150°C (1976°–2093°F)

Addition

(*a*) With tin oxide 6% replacing the copper oxide, a smooth opaque white glaze at 1080°C (1976°F); at 1150°C (2093°F) a rich iron speckle opaque over red clay.

85 Inky blue

Lead bisilicate	70
Flint	10
China clay	20
+ Manganese carbonate	3
Cobalt oxide	1

A rich inky blue glaze, shiny and smooth. 1080°–1150°C (1976°–2093°F)

3. Base and decorative glazes

86 A clear base glaze

Calcium borate frit (P2954) (Colemanite)	50
China clay	33
Flint	17

A clear base glaze, brighter at higher temperatures.

Additions

(*a*) With zirconium silicate 10%, white opaque results.
(*b*) With cobalt oxide 1% and nickel oxide 1%, a mid-opaque blue.

87 Good glaze base

Feldspar	20
Calcium borate frit (P2954) (Colemanite)	30
Borax frit (P2957)	14
Soda feldspar	15
Zinc oxide	5
China clay	14
Quartz	4

A semi-clear glaze at 1080°C (1976°F), slightly runny at 1150°C (2093°F).

Additions

(*a*) With tin oxide 6%, a smooth opaque white at 1080°C (1976°F); more lively at 1150°C (2093°F) with rich iron speckles over red clay.
(*b*) With iron oxide 8%, an opaque tan at 1080°C (1976°F); a rich dark brown orange at 1150°C (2093°F)
(*c*) With cobalt carbonate 2%, a midnight blue.
(*d*) With copper carbonate 3%, a mid-green develops.

88 Clear glaze base

Lead bisilicate	50
Borax frit (P2957)	20
Feldspar	10
Ball clay	15
Flint	5

A milky clear glaze at 1080°C (1976°F); clear at 1150°C (2093°F).

Additions

(*a*) With manganese carbonate 7%, a rich Rockingham brown results at 1080°C (1976°F); runny at 1150°C (2093°F).
(*b*) With iron oxide 4%, a semi-matt red brown at 1080°C (1976°F); a rich yellow red at 1150°C (2093°F).
(*c*) With green copper oxide 2%, a green results.

89 Matt base glaze

Lead bisilicate	70
Cornish (Cornwall) stone	10
Barium carbonate	10
China clay	10

A matt semi-opaque glaze at 1060°C (1940°F); clear at 1150°C (2093°F).

Additions

(*a*) With manganese carbonate 3%, a smooth matt purple brown at 1060°C (1940°F); a shiny pale brown at 1150°C (2093°F).
(*b*) With cobalt oxide 2%, a dark matt midnight blue.
(*c*) With copper oxide 3%, a smooth rich green at 1060°C (1940°F); runny at higher temperatures.

90 A clear crackle glaze

Alkaline frit (P2962)	70
Cornish (Cornwall) stone	20
China clay	10

A clear crackle at 1080°C (1976°F); transparent at 1150°C (2093°F).

91 Crystalline gold speckle

Lead bisilicate	50
Borax frit (P2957)	30
Rutile (light)	10
Zinc oxide	10

A crystalline glaze which, at higher temperatures, 1150°C (2093°F), gives a clear transparent with gold speckles on white body; runny, and the usual precautions with crystalline glazes need to be taken.

92 Clear base glaze

Lead bisilicate	65
Whiting	5
China clay	10
Flint	20

A clear base glaze at 1150°C (2093°F).

Additions

(*a*) With iron oxide 2%, a honey transparent results over white slip on white body.

(*b*). With iron oxide 3% and manganese dioxide 2%, a rich Rockingham brown.

(*c*). With cobalt oxide 1%, a midnight blue results.

1060°–1150°C (1940°–2093°F)

93 Opalescent

Alkaline frit (P2962)	86
Calcium borate frit (P2954) (Colemanite)	8
China clay	6

A bright opalescent blue with chun effects over red clays at higher temperatures. 1080°–1150°C (1976°–2093°F)

Additions

(*a*) With copper oxide 1.5%, a bright turquoise results.
(*b*) With cobalt oxide 1.5% and iron oxide 1%, a mid-blue results.
(*c*) With iron oxide 5%, a grey beige.

94 A mottled red green

Borax frit (P2957)	25
Alkaline frit (P2962)	14
Whiting	4
Zinc oxide	4
Lead bisilicate	30
China clay	10
Flint	13
+ Tin oxide	1
Copper carbonate	0.5
Silicon carbide	0.5

A local reduction copper red glaze which needs to soak to develop the colour. 1080°–1120°C (1976°–2048°F)

95 Mottled apple green

Calcium borate frit (P2954) (Colemanite)	5
Borax frit (P2957)	15
Alkaline frit (P2962)	15
Whiting	3
Zinc oxide	3
Lead bisilicate	30
China clay	10
Flint	19
+ Tin oxide	1
Copper carbonate	0.5
Silicon carbide	0.5

A mottled apple green glaze over light-coloured bodies. 1080°–1120°C (1976°–2048°F)

1150°–1200°C (2093°–2192°F) Orton cones 01–5

1. Clear, white matt and opaque glazes

96 A semi-clear glaze

Calcium borate frit (P2954) (Colemanite)	38
Whiting	7
Feldspar	36
Flint	15
Bentonite	4

A semi-clear glaze with chun streaky effect; over RS a matt pink blue chun effect results.

97 White opaque

Borax frit (P2957)	33
Lead bisilicate	40
Whiting	5
Feldspar	10
Tin oxide	9
Bentonite	3

A bright white opaque glaze, milky and rich. It is particularly attractive over red clay at higher temperatures when iron in body breaks through glaze with orange speckles. 1080°–1200°C (1976°–2192°F)

98 Semi-clear

Feldspar	35
Calcium borate frit (P2954) (Colemanite)	30
Zinc oxide	7
Barium carbonate	4
China clay	4
Flint	20

A semi-clear glaze at 1080°C (1976°F); a brighter chun type glaze at 1200°C (2192°F).

Addition

(*a*) With copper carbonate 2%, bright turquoise colours result.

99 White opaque glaze

Lead bisilicate	32
Borax frit (P2957)	46
China clay	22
+ Tin oxide	4

A high clay, white, opaque glaze at 1080°C (1976°F); richer and more milky at higher temperatures, 1200°C (2192°F).

100 Nickel red

Lead bisilicate	20
Nepheline syenite	16
Barium carbonate	35
Zinc oxide	15
China clay	4
Flint	10
+ Nickel oxide	2

A semi-matt pink red glaze, blue where thin.

1200°C (2192°F) Orton cone 5

1. Clear, white and opaque glazes

101 Clear glaze

Calcium borate frit (P2954) (Colemanite)	5
Borax frit (P2957)	30
Talc	10
Feldspar	45
Whiting	2
Barium carbonate	4
Bentonite	4

A clear transparent glaze.

102 Smooth clear glaze

Lead bisilicate	30
Feldspar	40
Zinc oxide	7
Whiting	12
Flint	6
China clay	5

A smooth bright glaze; do not apply thickly or overfire.

103 Clear

Feldspar	40
Whiting	10
Barium carbonate	5
Zinc oxide	10
Flint	30
China clay	5

A clear base glaze.

104 Clear

Alkaline frit (P2962)	35
Whiting	10
Dolomite	5
Feldspar	20
China clay	15
Flint	15

A clear glaze.

105 Clear transparent

Feldspar	60
Lead bisilicate	20
Whiting	10
Zinc oxide	5
China clay	5

A smooth transparent glaze; at higher temperatures a blue grey mottle over RS.

106 Clear glaze

Soda feldspar	40
Alkaline frit (P2962)	15
Lead bisilicate	25
Dolomite	8
China clay	5
Flint	7

A clear glaze, slightly orange over stoneware; at higher temperatures a tenmoku develops over IS, a black oil spot over BS.

107 Clear transparent

Lead bisilicate	45
Whiting	15
Feldspar	30
China clay	10

A clear transparent glaze; do not apply thickly.

108 A clear glaze

Feldspar	45
Whiting	20
Lead bisilicate	15
Borax frit (P2957)	10
Quartz	5
China clay	5

A clear base glaze, crazes if thickly applied; black blue over BS.

Addition

(*a*) With iron oxide 6%, a rich olive yellow results.

109 A milky stable glaze

Feldspar	44
Whiting	20
Lead bisilicate	14
Borax frit (P2957)	10
Quartz	6
China clay	6
+ Zirconium silicate	6

A semi-opaque white stable glaze.

110 Creamy glaze

Petalite	13
Wollastonite	11
Bone ash	4
Dolomite	27
Fremington clay	45
(Albany slip)	

A creamy white well-fluxed opaque glaze with ash-like effect. Attractive black green over BS; matt green black over GS; dark brown over YS.

111 Matt creamy white glaze

Lead bisilicate	20
Whiting	9
Dolomite	14
Feldspar	35
China clay	12
Titanium dioxide	10

A matt creamy white glaze.

112 A smooth slightly opaque glaze

Alkaline frit (P2962)	10
Lead bisilicate	16
Feldspar	25
Whiting	10
China clay	8
Flint	31

A smooth slightly opaque glaze. At 1260°C (2300°F) a blue black on BS.

113 Soft matt opaque

Lead bisilicate	40
Whiting	10
Barium carbonate	18
China clay	22
Flint	10

A smooth soft matt opaque glaze.

Additions

(*a*) With manganese dioxide 2%, a mauve purple develops.
(*b*) With copper oxide 2%, an attractive medium green.

114 Smooth dry cream matt

Feldspar	50
Whiting	20
Bone ash	4
Alkaline frit (P2962)	4
Talc	4
China clay	18

A smooth dry cream matt.

Addition

(*a*) With iron oxide 8%, a red ochre glaze develops.

115 Smooth matt

Alkaline frit (P2962)	50
Cornish (Cornwall) stone	30
Barium carbonate	10
Bentonite	5
Ball clay	5

A smooth semi-opaque matt glaze.

116 Semi-clear

Alkaline frit (P2962)	30
Whiting	3
Feldspar	25
China clay	15
Flint	27

A semi-clear smooth glaze over white body; a bubbly textured surface over red clay.

117 Smooth bright milky glaze/copper red

Borax frit (P2957)	13
Feldspar	50
Whiting	9
Flint	18
Zinc oxide	3
Ball clay	7

A smooth bright milky glaze, clearer at higher temperatures.

Additions

(*a*) With tin oxide 3%, a more opaque cooler white results.
(*b*) With tin oxide 2%, copper carbonate 0.5%, manganese carbonate 0.5%, silicon carbide 0.25%, a red speckle develops in a grey base.

118 Smooth beige grey glaze

Feldspar	42
Whiting	9
Barium carbonate	5
Zinc oxide	10
Flint	28
China clay	6
+ Chrome oxide	1

An opaque grey beige-coloured glaze.

119 A clear slightly speckled glaze

Feldspar	30
Whiting	20
Talc	10
Zinc oxide	10
Borax frit (P2957)	5
Titanium dioxide	3
China clay	12
Flint	10

A slightly speckled shiny glaze.

2. Coloured glazes

120 Smooth matt blue black

Feldspar	60
Borax frit (P2957)	10
Barium carbonate	18
China clay	12
+ Manganese carbonate	3
Cobalt oxide	2

A smooth opaque matt dark blue black.

121 Orange tan

Alkaline frit (P2962)	3
Whiting	10
Fremington clay (Albany slip)	67

A semi-matt orange tan glaze.

122 Medium brown glaze

Feldspar	44
Whiting	20
Lead bisilicate	14
Borax frit (P2957)	12
Quartz	5
China clay	5
+ Nickel oxide	2

A smooth medium brown glaze.

123 Oil spot effect

Cornish (Cornwall) stone	36
Nepheline syenite	44
Dolomite	10
China clay	10
+ Iron oxide	6

A smooth oil spot effect glaze; apply thickly.

124 Oil spot type glaze

Feldspar	20
Petalite	10
Barium carbonate	8
Talc	22
Fremington clay (Albany slip)	40
+ Iron oxide	5

A semi-matt brown black opaque with spots of lighter red; apply thickly.

125 Purplish brown glaze

Feldspar	44
Whiting	18
Lead bisilicate	14
Borax frit (P2957)	11
Quartz	6
China clay	7
+ Manganese dioxide	4

A purplish brown shiny glaze.

3. Decorative and textural glazes

126 Chun type glaze

Alkaline frit (P2962)	20
Calcium borate frit (P2954) (Colemanite)	10
Feldspar	50
Barium carbonate	3
Zinc oxide	3
Flint	14

A clear pale blue over white clay, a rich chun blue over red clay when applied thickly.

127 Opaque chun

Alkaline frit (P2962)	30
Zinc oxide	8
Whiting	12
Flint	35
China clay	15

A smooth opaque white glaze with rich blue chun effects over red clay.

128 Chun effect clear

Alkaline frit (P2962)	30
Feldspar	40
Whiting	5
China clay	5
Flint	20

A clear pale blue glaze, more opaque when applied thickly; over red clay an attractive blue chun results.

129 Chun glaze

Zinc oxide	10
Calcium borate frit (P2954) (Colemanite)	25
Quartz	10
China clay	5
Feldspar	50

A chun type glaze with opalescent blue markings.

Addition

(*a*) With cobalt oxide 1% and iron oxide 3%, a mottled green blue brown glaze develops.

130 Chun effect

Feldspar	42
Whiting	9
Barium carbonate	5
Zinc oxide	10
Flint	29
China clay	5
+ Rutile	5

A rich white chun effect glaze over red clay. A white opaque over white clay.

131 Matt nickel pink blue

Feldspar	68
Whiting	11
Zinc oxide	10
Barium carbonate	7
Bentonite	4
+ Nickel oxide	2

A matt pink blue glaze on stoneware.

132 Runny ash glaze

Talc	22
Alkaline frit (P2962)	23
Wood ash	48
Ball clay	7

A runny creamy yellow ash glaze.

133 Runny ash glaze

Calcium borate frit (P2954) (Colemanite)	12
Petalite	5
Whiting	20
Wood ash	20
Fremington clay (Albany slip)	43

A runny ash glaze, pale beige green, with typical ash break up.

Addition

(*a*) With iron oxide 3%, a richer colour develops.

134 A reactive honey glaze

Petalite	10
Barium carbonate	10
Calcium borate frit (P2954) (Colemanite)	15
Wollastonite	25
Fremington clay (Albany slip)	40

A runny honey-coloured glaze: orange green over VS

135 A crystalline glaze

Alkaline frit (P2962)	20
Borax frit (P2957)	17
Zinc oxide	26
Whiting	4
Quartz	30
Bentonite	3

A pale blue white crystalline glaze with bright crystal markings. Do not apply thickly as the glaze runs freely.

Additions

(*a*) With titanium dioxide 8%, opalescent blue greys develop.

(*b*) With titanium dioxide 8% and nickel oxide 2%, a bright pea green develops.

136 Textured crystalline glaze

Barium carbonate	20
Whiting	20
Zinc oxide	5
Lithium carbonate	6
China clay	10
Ball clay	9
Flint	30

A decorative crystalline matt glaze with crystal markings. Do not apply too thickly.

Additions

(*a*) With manganese carbonate 2%, a bright purple mauve colour.
(*b*) With iron oxide 3%, a broken yellow green colour.

137 Crystalline glaze

Alkaline frit (P2962)	25
Nepheline syenite	25
Barium carbonate	5
Zinc oxide	20
Flint	11
China clay	6
Titanium dioxide	8

A smooth creamy opaque with small orange tan crystals over stoneware body; a more pink colour over porcelain.

138 Clear crackle glaze

Nepheline syenite	67
Borax frit (P2957)	20
Whiting	10
Bentonite	3

A clear crackled glaze. Over dark body a more matt opaque surface results.

1200°–1220°C (2192°–2228°F) Orton cones 5–6

1. Clear, white and opaque glazes

139 A clear glaze

Feldspar	52
Zinc oxide	6
Whiting	20
China clay	5
Flint	17

A clear zinc glaze.

140 A smooth matt white

Cornish (Cornwall) stone	50
Whiting	10
Wood ash	40

A smooth matt white with soft iron speckles. Soft greens and tans over VS.

141 A semi-matt clear glaze

Lead bisilicate	30
Feldspar	30
Zinc oxide	4
Whiting	10
China clay	20
Flint	6

A semi-matt clear glaze 1200°C (2192°F); clearer at higher temperatures 1220°C (2228°F)

Addition

(*a*) With titanium dioxide 8%, opalescent blue greys develop.

(*b*) With titanium dioxide 8% and nickel oxide 2%, a bright pea green develops.

142 Chun type glaze

Cornish (Cornwall) stone	15
Barium carbonate	15
Talc	20
Whiting	10
Petalite	12
China clay	16
Flint	12

A transparent glaze with chun markings.

143 Textured clear glaze base

Borax frit (P2957)	28
China clay	28
Whiting	28
Quartz	16
+ Iron oxide	15

A slightly textured semi-matt glaze gives a brown ochre ash effect.

144 Decorative grey glaze with pink crystals

Soda feldspar	44
Borax frit (P2957)	30
Fluorspar	5
Flint	11
China clay	10
+ Zircon	6
Copper carbonate	0.75
Silcon carbide	1

A decorative dark grey glaze with pink crystals. The basic mixture is a smooth transparent glaze.

145 White bright glaze

Feldspar	37
Whiting	12
Zinc oxide	18
China clay	26
Flint	7

A smooth white opaque glaze.

Addition
With cobalt oxide 0.5%, copper oxide 1% and manganese 1%, a medium soft blue glaze results.

146 White frosty glaze

Feldspar	36
Alkaline frit (P2962)	9
Whiting	14
Barium carbonate	21
Zinc oxide	3
China clay	7
Flint	10

A smooth semi-matt frosty glaze.

Additions

(*a*) With nickel oxide 1.5%, a brown base with mauve-coloured markings.
(*b*) With chrome oxide 0.5%, a bright luminescent pea green develops.

147 A matt textured glaze

Talc	62
Fluorspar	33
Bentonite	5
+ Iron oxide	5

A curious glaze, suitable for sculptural forms, matt rich chocolate brown with textural markings.

148 Mottled black brown

Calcium borate frit (P2954) (Colemanite)	15
Petalite	15
Fremington clay (Albany slip)	70

A smooth black brown glaze with mottled texture.

Addition

(*a*) With iron oxide 3%, a darker brown glaze results.

149 Clear glaze

Borax frit (P2957)	30
Whiting	20
Quartz	20
China clay	30

A clear glaze base with some slightly broken texturing.

Addition

(*a*) With red iron oxide 10%, a bright orange tan develops on porcelain, darker on stoneware.

150 Broken ochre-coloured glaze

Whiting	25
China clay	20
Ball clay	20
Flint	35
+ Crocus martis	4
Rutile	5

A smooth semi-matt ochre-coloured glaze breaking a darker tan.

1200°–1260°C
2192°–2300°F
Orton cone 5–8

1. Clear, white, matt, opaque and semi-clear glazes

151 Clear glaze

Feldspar	40
Whiting	16
Talc	2
Zinc oxide	4
Quartz	30
China clay	8

A clear well-fitting smooth glaze. 1220°–1260°C (2228°–2300°F)

152 Clear base glaze

Nepheline syenite	30
Whiting	15
Talc	5
Zinc oxide	5
Ball clay	10
Flint	35

A smooth clear base glaze over a wide temperature range, slightly opalescent in reduction.

Addition

(*a*) With tin oxide 6%, a smooth bright opaque white.
(*b*) With rutile 4%, an opalescent/white bright glaze, with pinkish tinge in reduction.

153 Clear base glaze

Whiting	7
Feldspar	35
Barium carbonate	8
Zinc oxide	10
China clay	6
Ball clay	6
Flint	28

A smooth well-fitting transparent glaze over a wide temperature range.

Additions

(*a*) With copper carbonate 1.5%, a soft medium green develops.
(*b*) With nickel oxide 1%, a medium brown.

154 Transparent glaze

Barium carbonate	7
Feldspar	65
Whiting	7
Zinc oxide	9
Ball clay	9
Flint	23

A smooth bright clear glaze. 1200°–1250°C (2192°–2282°F)

155 Clear chun type glaze

Zinc oxide	3
Barium carbonate	6
Calcium borate frit (P2954) (Colemanite)	20
Whiting	2
Feldspar	45
China clay	4
Flint	20

A clear glaze with a milky-chun quality if applied thickly over RS and YS.

Additions

(*a*) With chrome oxide 0.5%, an opaque pinky beige results.

(*b*) With nickel oxide 1.5% and cobalt carbonate 0.5%, a mottled grey blue develops.

156 Chun type clear glaze (oxidation)

Feldspar	52
Wollastonite	22
Zinc oxide	5
Quartz	18
Bentonite	3

A smooth clear glaze when thin; chun-like blue white opacity when thicker in oxidation. Do not overfire. Intense colour response from BS (black blue), IS (brown black).

Additions

(*a*) With copper oxide 1.5%, pale turquoise, delicate over porcelain (oxidation).

(*b*) With cobalt oxide 0.5% and nickel oxide 1%, bright blue/green (oxidation).

157 Shiny chun type

Feldspar	40
Zinc oxide	12
Whiting	14
China clay	6
Quartz	28

A shiny semi-transparent stable glaze with blue white flecks on porcelain and stoneware. Good over slips: blue black over BS, pale green over GS, blue grey over IS, red blue over RS; darker at 1260°C (2300°F).

Additions

(*a*) With titanium dioxide 4%, a whiter more opaque glaze develops at 1200°C (2192°F). At 1260°C (2300°F) a darker blue black mottled effect results.

(*b*) With titanium dioxide 8% and nickel oxide 1.5%, an opaque pale green develops.

158 Chun type glaze

Calcium borate frit (P2954) (Colemanite)	55
Feldspar	10
China clay	15
Flint	20
+ Zirconium silicate	12

A clear glaze with opaque blue white markings rather like the classical Chinese chun glaze. 1200°–1220°C (2192°–2228°F)

159 A smooth clear glaze

Feldspar	38
Whiting	15
Barium carbonate	7
Zinc oxide	4
Flint	23
China clay	13

A good smooth clear wide temperature glaze.

Additions

(*a*) With zirconium silicate 12%, a smooth opaque white develops in oxidation and reduction.

(*b*) With vanadium pentoxide 3%, a pink brown glaze develops in oxidation.

160 A frosty clear glaze

Alkaline frit (P2962)	17
Barium carbonate	17
Whiting	7
Feldspar	30
China clay	7
Flint	22

A slightly matt, frosty glaze at 1200°C (2192°F); clearer at 1260°C (2300°F); soft lovat green over GS at 1200°C (2192°F).

161 Clear transparent

Alkaline frit (P2962)	25
Dolomite	20
Feldspar	25
Ball clay	25
Flint	5

A wide range clear glaze, smooth and craze-free. Mottled black brown over IS; blue black over BS at 1200°C (2192°F). At 1260°C (2300°F) rich iron browns over IS, black brown over YS.

162 A clear smooth transparent glaze

Alkaline frit (P2962)	20
Dolomite	25
Feldspar	20
Ball clay	25
Flint	10

At 1200°C (2192°F) a smooth, semi-clear glaze, transparent at 1260°C (2300°F). Over YS, at 1200°C (2192°F) a dark mottled matt, at 1260°C (2300°F) rich iron rust tenmoku.

163 Bright transparent

Nepheline syenite	37
Barium carbonate	3
Calcium borate frit (P2954) (Colemanite)	3
Dolomite	6
Whiting	10
Zinc oxide	5
China clay	8
Flint	28

A bright clear transparent, crazes if applied thickly.

Addition

(*a*) With tin oxide 3%, a milky white transparent glaze results.

164 A clear glaze

Feldspar	48
Zinc oxide	7
Barium carbonate	3
Dolomite	4
Whiting	5
China clay	10
Flint	23

A clear glaze with a soft pleasant surface.

Additions

(*a*) With cobalt oxide 0.5% and nickel oxide 0.5%, a pleasant medium blue results.

(*b*) With copper oxide 2%, a medium bright green glaze.

165 A clear transparent glaze

Feldspar	48
Calcium borate frit (P2954) (Colemanite)	10
Barium carbonate	12
Zinc oxide	4
Whiting	10
Flint	10
Ball clay	6

A bright clear transparent glaze, do not apply thickly. Over IS a rich tenmoku develops at higher temperatures.

Addition

(*a*) With copper carbonate 2%, a bright watery green results.

166 A clear wide temperature glaze

Talc	5
Alkaline frit (P2962)	30
Feldspar	35
Whiting	15
China clay	6
Flint	9

A smooth clear wide temperature glaze; will craze if thickly applied.

167 A clear base glaze

Feldspar	50
Zinc oxide	10
Whiting	15
China clay	5
Flint	20

A clear base glaze, smooth at 1220°C (2228°F). An attractive pale blue in reduction at 1260°C (2300°F).

Addition

(*a*) With tin oxide 6%, a deep milky white opaque glaze results.

168 A frosty craze-free glaze

Cornish (Cornwall) stone	44
Calcium borate frit (P2954) (Colemanite)	6
Dolomite	10
Whiting	10
Flint	10
China clay	20

A wide-ranging frosty crackle-free glaze, more matt at 1220°C (2228°F), a clear pale blue in reduction. Mottled brown grey over IS in oxidation, iron tenmoku over YS and IS in reduction. 1220°–1260°C (2228°–2300°F).

Additions

(*a*) With iron oxide 2%, a pale matt cream develops in oxidation, a muted celadon in reduction.

(*b*) With copper oxide 2%, a semi-matt mid-green results in oxidation, a good pink in reduction.

169 Soft semi-matt glaze

Feldspar	30
Nepheline syenite	10
Whiting	30
Ball clay	30

Soft semi-matt glaze in oxidation and reduction, drier over stoneware. Dry speckle at 1200°C (2192°F). Good over all slips especially BS. In reduction green tenmoku over IS/YS.

Additions

(*a*) With iron oxide 4%, an attractive semi-matt brown yellow in oxidation, dark green and runny in reduction. Ochre green speckle at 1200°C (2192°F).

(*b*) With iron oxide 8%, ochre-coloured variations in oxidation and reduction.

170 A semi-clear glaze

Alkaline frit (P2962)	15
Dolomite	25
Feldspar	20
Ball clay	20
Flint	20

A smooth semi-clear glaze at 1200°C (2192°F), more transparent at 1260°C (2300°F). At 1200°C (2192°F) mottled brown and white eggshell patterns over YS. At 1260°C (2300°F) a smooth iron brown over IS, darker over YS.

171 Semi-clear glaze

Feldspar	50
Calcium borate frit (P2954) (Colemanite)	6
Dolomite	8
Whiting	8
Flint	10
China clay	18

A wide-ranging semi-clear glaze in oxidation; an attractive iron speckle in reduction. Mottled blue brown over BS in oxidation, red and grey over IS, YS in reduction.

Additions

(*a*) With iron oxide 8%, a shiny tenmoku in reduction, more matt in oxidation.
(*b*) With copper oxide 2%, mid-greens develop in oxidation, pinks in reduction.

172 Smooth semi-clear glaze

Soda feldspar	38
Alkaline frit (P2962)	30
Whiting	10
China clay	16
Flint	6

A smooth semi-clear glaze. A rich red brown over YS, a green brown over IS.

173 Clear bright and speckled glaze

Calcium borate frit (P2954) (Colemanite)	20
Alkaline frit (P2962)	15
Feldspar	15
Petalite	10
China clay	15
Flint	25

A clear bright transparent glaze.
Particularly attractive with an addition of tin oxide 6% which gives white opaque glaze, which develops attractive speckles over stoneware.

174 Semi-matt glaze

Spodumene	35
Whiting	22
Flint	30
China clay	13

A semi-matt glaze at 1200°C (2192°F). Over IS a green black mottled effect at 1260°C (2300°F).

175 A semi-matt white opaque

Nepheline syenite	45
Petalite	13
Dolomite	26
Flint	5
Ball clay	6
China clay	5
+ Tin oxide	2

A semi-matt white glaze, breaking orange over stoneware, and giving a more shino-like effect at 1260°C (2300°F) (electric kiln). Over BS a rich white with dark brown texture at 1200°C (2192°F). At 1260°C (2300°F) slip reaction is much more active.

176 A frosty satin glaze

Nepheline syenite	35
Whiting	25
Ball clay	15
Flint	25

A smooth satin white on porcelain, more frosty in oxidation, a clear glaze in reduction. Mottled brown ochre over IS, a blue black over BS in oxidation. Iron green over YS, pink red over GS in reduction. 1220°–1260°C (2228°–2300°F).

Addition
With copper carbonate 2%, frosty greens develop in oxidation, muted pink in reduction.

177 Matt white

Feldspar	45
Whiting	18
Zinc oxide	10
China clay	18
Flint	9

A smooth matt white at 1200°C (2192°F), slightly more runny at 1260°C (2300°F).

178 Matt white

Feldspar	48
Zinc oxide	7
Whiting	18
Calcium borate frit (P2954) (Colemanite)	6
China clay	16
Flint	5

A smooth matt white glaze at 1200°C (2192°F); over BS blue black; over GS pale green; over RS pale cream green; over YS mottled coffee brown. At 1260°C (2300°F) glaze and slip response is more pronounced.

179 Soft matt speckled white

Feldspar	50
Zinc oxide	10
Whiting	20
China clay	14
Flint	6

A smooth attractive soft white with delicate iron speckling at 1200°C (2192°F); good slip response. At 1260°C (2300°F) this glaze is more runny and less smooth.

180 Smooth matt

Feldspar	25
Petalite	25
Dolomite	25
Ball clay	25

A smooth semi-opaque matt at 1200°C (2192°F). Over YS a dark brown mottle results. Glaze becomes clearer at higher temperatures – 1260°C (2300°F).

181 A viscous opaque white

Feldspar	75
Whiting	8
Bone ash	7
China clay	5
Flint	5

A smooth deep opaque white, with a tendency to crackle when applied thickly. 1220°–1260°C (2228°–2300°F)

Addition

(*a*) With cobalt oxide 0.75% and nickel oxide 1%, dark grey blue opaque results.

182 Semi-opaque base glaze

Nepheline syenite	73
Zinc oxide	3
Magnesium carbonate	3
Whiting	3
China clay	10
Flint	8

A smooth semi-opaque base glaze, particularly attractive in reduction.

Additions

(*a*) With copper carbonate 1%, a pinky green develops at 1220°C (2228°F). At higher temperatures (1260°C [2230°F]) a mottled ochre green develops in reduction; a clearer green in oxidation.

(*b*) With copper carbonate 0.5% and rutile 3%, a rich sea-green broken blue develops at all temperatures.

183 Smooth semi-opaque white

Feldspar	50
Dolomite	10
Calcium borate frit (P2954) (Colemanite)	10
Whiting	10
China clay	20

A smooth semi-opaque white.

Addition

(*a*) With tin oxide 4%, an opaque white breaking orange at higher temperatures.

184 Semi-opaque glaze

Feldspar	25
Petalite	25
Dolomite	25
Calcium borate frit (P2954) (Colemanite)	3
China clay	10
Flint	12

A frosty semi-opaque glaze at 1200°C (2192°F), clearer at 1260°C (2300°F). Over YS a brown mottle develops at 1200°C (2192°F).

Additions

a) With zirconium silicate 6%, a flat opaque white at 1200°C (2192°F), less opaque at 1260°C (2300°F).

b) With tin oxide 4%, an opaque white at 1200°F (2192°F), a lively bright white with orange speckles at 1260°C (2300°F).

185 Smooth opaque white

Zinc oxide	20
Feldspar	35
Whiting	12
China clay	25
Flint	8

A smooth opaque white at 1200°C (2192°F). At 1260°C (2300°F) the glaze is more shiny and on porcelain will tend to form crystals.

186 A creamy white opaque

Feldspar	50
Whiting	22
Zinc oxide	4
China clay	20
Quartz	4

At 1200°C (2192°F) a smooth creamy white matt; brown speckled white over IS; drier cream brown over YS; soft greens over GS. At 1260°C (2300°F) a drier matt.

Additions

(*a*) With iron oxide 3% and rutile 3%, a creamy yellow breaking at 1260°C (2300°F), more restrained at 1200°C (2192°F).

(*b*) With cobalt carbonate 0.75%, nickel oxide 0.5%, manganese carbonate 1.5% and iron oxide 1%, a dark grey blue develops.

187 Smooth opaque glaze

Petalite	39
Whiting	32
Flint	18
China clay	11

At 1200°C (2192°F) a smooth opaque semi-matt; at 1260°C (2300°F) transparent.

Addition

(*a*) With iron oxide 5%, a smooth speckled orange brown develops at 1200°C (2192°F); more runny at 1260°C (2300°F).

188 Smooth opaque matt

Soda feldspar	50
Dolomite	20
Whiting	5
Talc	5
China clay	20

A smooth opaque white in oxidation, a more satin surface in reduction. Black brown cream over IS, brown mottled over YS in oxidation. 1220°–1260°C (2228°–2300°F).

Additions

(*a*) With tin oxide 6%, a white with orange flashing results in oxidation.

(*b*) With tin oxide 4% and copper oxide 1.5%, a green glaze with orange flashing results, a muted mauve pink in reduction.

189 Stiff white semi-opaque

Feldspar	30
Whiting	18
Barium carbonate	4
Quartz	36
China clay	12

A stiff semi-opaque glaze, creamy in oxidation, more grey blue in reduction. 1220°–1260°C (2228°–2300°F)

Addition

(*a*) With zirconium silicate 10%, a smooth opaque white develops.

190 Semi-matt white glaze

Soda feldspar	80
Whiting	10
Zinc oxide	6
China clay	4
+ Bone ash	3

A frosty matt in oxidation, a clearer satin in reduction. In reduction a mottled iron black over YS. At 1200°C (2192°F) a soft mottled semi-matt speckled white. Attractive green black crystalline results over GS.

191 A semi-clear glaze

Petalite	38
Whiting	32
Flint	18
China clay	12

A semi-clear glaze at 1200°C (2192°F), more shiny at 1260°C (2300°F). A shiny celadon green breaking rust over IS at 1260°C (2300°F).

192 Smooth semi-clear glaze

Petalite	38
Whiting	19
Flint	32
China clay	11

A smooth semi-clear glaze at 1200°C (2192°F), transparent and craze-free at 1260°C (2300°F). Rich iron rusts over VS at 1260°C (2300°F).

Additions

(*a*) With tin oxide 2%, a smooth milky white glaze results.
(*b*) With tin oxide 4%, a more opaque glaze results.

193 Semi-opaque

Feldspar	60
Zinc oxide	6
Whiting	12
China clay	10
Flint	12

A smooth semi-opaque glaze at 1200°C (2192°F); a clear glaze at 1260°C (2300°F). Over BS at 1260°C (2300°F) a blue black results.

194 A semi-clear chun glaze

Alkaline frit (P2962)	15
Feldspar	39
Dolomite	5
Whiting	8
Zinc oxide	5
China clay	6
Flint	22

A semi-clear glaze with pale blue chun effect at 1200°C (2192°F); clearer at 1260°C (2300°F). Pale lovat green over GS; deep at 1200°C (2192°F); blue black over YS and BS at 1260°C (2300°F).

195 Clear bright and speckled glaze

Calcium borate frit (P2954) (Colemanite)	20
Alkaline frit (P2962)	15
Feldspar	15
Petalite	10
Flint	25
China clay	15

A clear bright transparent glaze.

(a) Particularly attractive with an addition of tin oxide 6%, which gives a white opaque glaze which develops attractive speckles over stoneware.

2. Coloured glazes

196 Soft green

Lepidolite	38
Flint	25
Whiting	22
China clay	15
+ Copper oxide	2

A medium soft green with black flecks at 1200°C (2192°F).

197 Brilliant matt turquoise (oxidation)

Barium carbonate	54
Spodumene	43
Bentonite	3
+ Copper carbonate	3

A brilliant turquoise matt glaze, smooth and bright.

(*a*) Without the copper carbonate this glaze gives a dry white with soft pink markings.

198 Mauve blue matt glaze

Nepheline syenite	34
Dolomite	16
Zinc oxide	5
Whiting	7
China clay	18
Bentonite	2
+ Copper oxide	0.5
Cobalt oxide	1

A smooth matt bright mauve breaking blue in oxidation; a darker midnight blue in reduction. 1220°–1260°C (2228°–2300°F)

199 Smooth blue grey

Feldspar	31
Dolomite	29
Whiting	6
China clay	29
Flint	5
+ Tin oxide	2
Copper carbonate	1.5

A smooth matt pale grey green at 1220°C (2228°F); a speckled pale blue green at 1260°C (2300°F) on porcelain.

200 Soft blue grey

Feldspar	40
Wood ash	40
China clay	10
Flint	10
+ Nickel oxide	0.5
Cobalt carbonate	0.5
Titanium dioxide	2

A soft smooth blue glaze at 1200°C (2192°F), more shiny at 1260°C (2300°F).

201 Rutile mottled glaze

Feldspar	70
Whiting	10
Zinc oxide	10
Barium carbonate	7
Bentonite	3
+ Rutile	5

A smooth matt on stoneware at 1220°C (2228°F), a shiny pale blue pink at 1260°C (2300°F) in oxidation, a dark blue grey with pink pooling in reduction.

(*a*) Without the rutile a rich mottled grey blue develops on RS in oxidation.

1200°–1260°C (2192°–2300°F)

202 Turquoise matt glaze

Barium carbonate	30
Nepheline syenite	50
Lithium carbonate	1
Ball clay	8
Flint	11
+ Copper carbonate	3

A smooth matt deep turquoise in oxidation, a pinky green in reduction. 1220°–1260°C (2228°–2300°F)

Additions

(*a*) With ilmenite 3%, a greener glaze develops in oxidation.

(*b*) With nickel oxide 2% replacing the copper carbonate, a matt purple results.

203 Turquoise green (oxidation)

Barium carbonate	36
Lithium carbonate	2
Nepheline syenite	58
Ball clay	4
+ Copper oxide	2

A matt deep turquoise green glaze. Do not overfire. Good on stoneware and porcelain. 1200°–1250°C (2192°–2282°F)

204 Yellow amber glaze (oxidation)

Talc	30
Petalite	20
Whiting	25
Flint	25
Bentonite	3

A semi-matt yellow amber glaze where thick, more textured where applied more thickly. 1250°–1260°C (2282°–2300°F)

205 Opaque ash-type glaze

Nepheline syenite	14
Dolomite	32
Whiting	15
Zinc oxide	7
China clay	12
Flint	20

An opaque ash-type glaze; do not apply too thickly as the markings become very runny. 1200°–1220°C (2192°–2228°F)

206 Mottled blue

Cornish stone	58
Whiting	35
China clay	7
+ Cobalt carbonate	1
Rutile (light)	3

A mottled pale blue, darker blue where thin, when fired to higher temperatures; an attractive transparent midnight blue develops. 1200°–1220°C (2192°–2228°F)

207 Tan matt

Feldspar	25
Petalite	5
Zinc oxide	5
Barium carbonate	5
Bone ash	5
Dolomite	12
Fremington clay (Albany slip)	43

A smooth matt tan-coloured glaze. 1200°C (2192°F)

208 Purple glaze

Feldspar	40
Petalite	16
Barium carbonate	28
China clay	9
Flint	9
+ Nickel oxide	1

A matt purple glaze develops in oxidation and reduction. 1220°–1260°C (2228°–2300°F)

209 Grey pink

Nepheline syenite	65
Dolomite	7
Zinc oxide	4
Whiting	5
China clay	7
Flint	10
Bentonite	2
+ Rutile (light)	6
Copper carbonate	2

A smooth matt grey pink glaze. 1220°–1260°C (2228°–2300°F)

Addition

(*a*) With vanadium pentoxide 4%, instead of the rutile and copper a bright matt pea green develops.

210 Matt speckled brown ochre-coloured glaze

Fremington clay (Albany slip)	50
Whiting	25
Feldspar	5
China clay	20

An attractive mottled brown ochre-coloured glaze.

Addition

(*a*) With iron oxide 2%, a darker and more mottled glaze results.

211 Red brown semi-shiny glaze

Wood ash	35
Feldspar	10
Whiting	5
Flint	20
Yellow ochre	20
China clay	10

A glaze which works well over a wide temperature range, giving a more matt effect at the lower temperatures (1220°C [2228°F]), more shiny in reduction. In reduction good iron tenmokus over YS, IS and RS. In oxidation attractive mottled red brown over IS and RS, greener over BS and GS. At 1220°C (2228°F), brown red mottled results over GS and IS.

Additions

a) With iron oxide 2%, more reddish in oxidation, more shiny in reduction.

b) With cobalt oxide 1%, deep grey blue matt glazes develop in oxidation, rich green brown black in reduction.

1200°–1260°C (2192°–2300°F)

212 Rich olive green (reduction)

Petalite	5
Dolomite	25
Wollastonite	15
Fremington clay (Albany slip)	55

An attractive dark green semi-shiny glaze with mottle in reduction; a satin matt pale green in oxidation at 1200°C (2192°F) and 1260°C (2300°F). A dark iron brown over IS at 1200°C (2192°F).

213 Shiny green with black crystals

Nepheline syenite	38
Whiting	28
Flint	21
China clay	13
+ Copper oxide	1.5

A shiny mid-green glaze with black crystal formations in oxidation; a pinky green in reduction at 1240°C (2264°F).

(*a*) Without the copper oxide but with tin oxide 4%, an opaque creamy white develops on porcelain in oxidation; in reduction a pale blue green.

214 Bright transparent green

Nepheline syenite	30
Whiting	14
Barium carbonate	14
Zinc oxide	3
Ball clay	6
Flint	33
+ Copper carbonate	1.5

A smooth bright transparent green glaze; do not overfire or apply too thickly.

(*a*) If 1.5% manganese carbonate is substituted for the copper carbonate, a mauve brown glaze results. 1200°–1250°C (2192°–2282°F)

215 Indian red

Feldspar	40
Zinc oxide	4
Dolomite	3
Whiting	15
China clay	5
Flint	33
+ Chrome oxide	0.5
Iron oxide	4

A rich bright Indian red over a wide temperature range.

216 Rich red mottle

Feldspar	55
Talc	9
Bone ash	9
China clay	9
Flint	18
+ Iron oxide	8

A smooth bright rich red mottled glaze in oxidation and reduction.

217 Soft dove pink

Zinc oxide	5
Nepheline syenite	35
Dolomite	15
Whiting	7
China clay	20
Flint	18
+ Copper oxide	2

A soft pinky grey matt glaze; darker in reduction. 1220°–1260°C (2228°–2300°F)

218 An opaque pink glaze

Nepheline syenite	26
Whiting	12
Lithium carbonate	10
Barium carbonate	3
Calcium borate frit (P2954) (Colemanite)	5
Flint	44

An opaque smooth bright pink glaze at 1200°C (2192°F), more muted at 1260°C (2300°F).

Addition

(*a*) With tin oxide 4% and rutile 3%, a pink white glaze results.

219 Chrome pink

Feldspar	50
Whiting	30
Flint	5
China clay	15
+ Tin oxide	4
Chrome oxide	0.2

A matt dusty pink at 1200°C (2192°F), shinier and slightly more runny at 1260°C (2300°F), brighter on porcelain.

(*a*) At 1260°C (2300°F) the base glaze without the colouring oxides gives an attractive blue black over BS, a brown cream over YS.

220 Smooth matt light mustard yellow

Nepheline syenite	10
Petalite	5
Bone ash	6
Wollastonite	24
Zinc oxide	5
Fremington clay (Albany slip)	50

A smooth, slightly mottled mustard green glaze, more runny at 1260°C (2300°F). Soft green over GS at 1200°C (2192°F).

Addition

(*a*) With copper oxide 2%, a soft matt green results at 1200°C (2192°F), more runny and broken at 1260°C (2300°F).

221 Pale clear honey

Feldspar	28
Petalite	5
Barium carbonate	7
Calcium borate frit (P2954) (Colemanite)	18
Alkaline frit (P2962)	20
Fremington clay (Albany slip)	22

A pale clear honey glaze, colour more intense at 1260°C (2300°F). At 1200°C (2192°F) olive brown over YS, darker at 1260°C (2300°F). Dark green brown over IS, red brown over YS at 1260°C (2300°F).

Addition

(*a*) With iron oxide 5%, a darker olive green glaze results at 1200°C (2192°F); a tenmoku on stoneware at 1260°C (2300°F).

222 Bright pale tan

Zinc oxide	5
Petalite	5
Bone ash	5
Dolomite	20
Flint	20
Fremington clay (Albany slip)	45

A smooth bright pale orange tan over a wide range.

223 Pale orange brown matt

Dolomite	20
Petalite	10
Bone ash	3
Wollastonite	12
Red clay	55

A smooth matt ochre-coloured glaze at 1200°C (2192°F) and 1260°C (2300°F), in oxidation; a speckled dark semi-matt green in reduction at 1260°C (2300°F).

224 Matt red brown

Feldspar	24
Cornish (Cornwall) stone	8
Whiting	26
China clay	22
Ball clay	5
Flint	15
+ Iron oxide	8

A smooth matt yellow brown at 1200°C (2192°F), darker and more broken at 1260°C (2300°F).

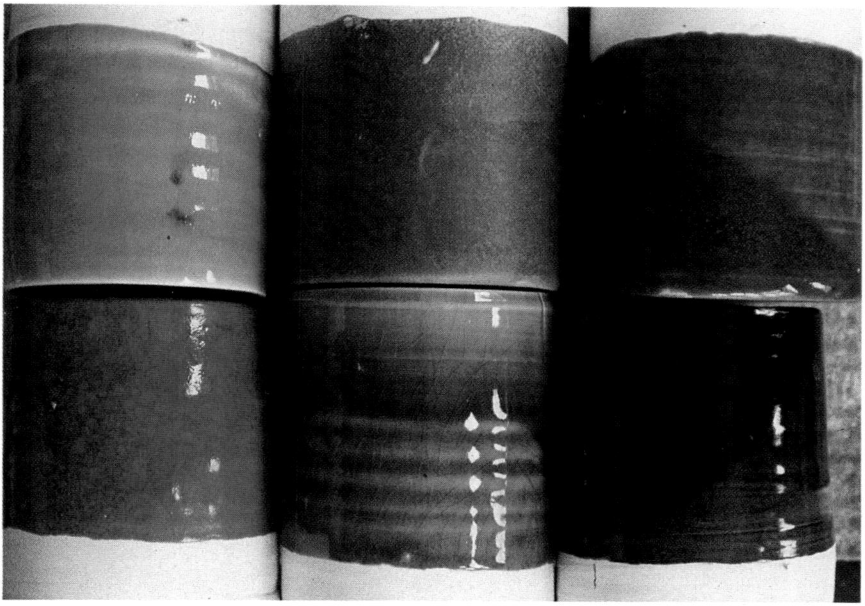

Blue and green earthenware glazes fired on white body at 1060°-1080°C (1940°-1976°F)
Top row 93a, 89c, 84
Bottom row 93b, 24, 85

Earthenware glazes fired at 1060°-1080°C (1940°-1976°F)
Top row 31 (white body), 84 (red body), 88a (white body)
Bottom row 19 (red body), 45b (white body), 93 (red body)

Medium temperature glazes fired on light-coloured body at 1200°-1220°C (2192°-2228°F)
Top row 243a, 245b, 234a, 186b
Bottom row 234g, 241 (fired to 1260°C [2300°F]), 241, 197

Medium temperature glazes fired on light-coloured body at 1200°-1220°C (2192°-2228°F)
Top row 234, 234e, 200, 331a, 141b
Bottom row 218a, 156a, 178, 234h, 113b

Medium temperature glazes fired on stoneware clay at 1200°-1220°C (2192°-2228°F)
Top row 242c, 157a, 157 over BS
Bottom row 233a, 190, 157 over RS

Glazes on stoneware clay fired to 1260°C (2300°F) in electric kiln
Top row 114 over YS, 141b, 378b
Bottom row 234e, 215, 377 with iron oxide

Glazes over stoneware clay fired to 1260°C (2300°F) in electric kiln
Top row 241b, 323, 186a
Bottom row 197, 243a, 378 over RS

lazes fired over stoneware clay to 1260°C
300°F) in gas-fired reduction kiln
p row 295 over GS, 409a, 410, 188
ottom row 344, 394 over BS, 387 over BS, 245b

lazes fired over stoneware clay to 1260°C
300°F) in gas-fired kiln
p row 245 over RS, 188 over BS, 293
ottom row 344a, 387 over YS, 409b

Glazes fired over porcelain clay to 1260°C
(2300°F) in gas-fired kiln
Top row 344, 282a, 188, 410, 245b
Bottom row 409, 344, 245c, 156b, 245a

Glazes fired to 1260°C (2300°F) in electric kiln
Top row 396 (stoneware body), 202 (porcelain body), 391 (porcelain body), 396 (porcelain body)
Bottom row 371 (porcelain body), 242b (stoneware body), 396 over painted iron oxide (stoneware body), 391 (porcelain body)

225 Brown black

Petalite	15
Calcium borate frit (P2954) (Colemanite)	10
Alkaline frit (P2962)	15
Fremington clay (Albany slip)	60

A smooth black brown glaze, hare's fur effect over YS at 1220°C (2228°F). Light-coloured tenmoku over IS at 1260°C (2300°F).

226 Semi-matt black brown

Feldspar	10
Calcium borate frit (P2954) (Colemanite)	3
Petalite	5
Talc	9
Fremington clay (Albany slip)	73

At 1200°C (2192°F) a smooth semi-matt black brown; at 1260°C (2300°F) a more shiny dark red brown. At 1260°C (2300°F) good tenmoku over IS; lighter tenmoku over RS; mottled red brown over YS.

227 Black slip glaze

Alkaline frit (P2962)	10
Fremington clay (Albany slip)	90
+ Cobalt oxide	3

A smooth dense silky black slip glaze.

228 Iron tenmoku

Petalite	15
Alkaline frit (P2962)	10
Calcium borate frit (P2954) (Colemanite)	10
Bone ash	3
Fremington clay (Albany slip)	62

A smooth mottled brown black at 1200°C (2192°F), less mottled at 1260°C (2300°F). At 1200°C (2192°F) a hare's fur type glaze over YS, at 1260°C (2300°F) a bright tenmoku. Over IS a tenmoku at 1260°C (2300°F).

Addition

(*a*) With iron oxide 5%, a tenmoku-type glaze at 1200°C (2192°F), more even brown at 1260°C (2300°F).

229 Honey base for tenmoku

Feldspar	20
Petalite	5
Dolomite	8
Calcium borate frit (P2954) (Colemanite)	7
Alkaline frit (P2962)	14
Fremington clay (Albany slip)	46

A clear honey glaze, darker on stoneware body than porcelain at 1200°C (2192°F). At 1260°C (2300°F) a good black brown tenmoku on IS, more mottled on RS.

Addition

(*a*) With iron oxide 5%, good smooth tenmokus at 1200°C (2192°F), blacker on porcelain. At 1260°C (2300°F) a more even brown.

230 Smooth black brown

Borax frit (P2957)	10
Alkaline frit (P2962)	10
Fremington clay	80

A smooth black brown slip glaze; the surface is brighter over porcelain.

Addition

(*a*) With cobalt carbonate 1% and iron oxide 2%, a darker glaze develops with an oil spot effect at lower temperatures, brighter at higher temperatures.

3. Base glazes

231 Clear basic glaze

Feldspar	40
Barium carbonate	5
Zinc oxide	5
Whiting	15
Quartz	25
China clay	10

A clear transparent glaze, creamy in oxidation, more blue in reduction. 1200°–1250°C (2192°–2282°F)

Additions

(*a*) With nickel oxide 2%, a coffee brown develops in oxidation, a grey in reduction.

(*b*) With vanadium pentoxide 3%, a mottled blue cream develops in oxidation, a mottled blue grey in reduction.

232 Transparent base

Dolomite	10
Calcium borate frit (P2954) (Colemanite)	11
Whiting	10
Cornish (Cornwall) stone	40
China clay	20
Flint	9

A wide-ranging clear glaze in oxidation, slightly blue in reduction. 1220°–1260°C (2228°–2300°F)

Additions

(*a*) With iron oxide 2%, a honey speckle results in oxidation, a pale celadon in reduction.

(*b*) With iron oxide 8%, a semi-matt tenmoku develops in oxidation, more shiny in reduction.

(*c*) With copper oxide 2%, a green speckled glaze results in oxidation, a good mid-pink in reduction.

(*d*) With cobalt carbonate 1%, a medium blue develops.

(*e*) With chrome oxide 0.5%, muted brown speckled glazes result.

(*f*) With zirconium silicate 6%, a semi-opaque white develops.

(*g*) With tin oxide 6%, a white with orange speckle develops in oxidation, a smooth white in reduction.

233 A clear transparent glaze

Feldspar	44
Barium carbonate	6
Calcium borate frit (P2954) (Colemanite)	20
Whiting	2
China clay	5
Flint	23

A stable transparent glaze. Over IS a rich black brown results, with tenmoku effects at 1260°C (2300°F).
Over YS a blue chun glaze results.

Additions

(*a*) With zinc oxide 3%, copper oxide 3%, rutile 1%, a semi-opaque mottled green results.
(*b*) With zinc oxide 3%, tin oxide 6%, cobalt oxide 2%, rutile 3%, a semi-opaque green blue results.
(*c*) With zinc oxide 3%, manganese carbonate 5%, rutile 2%, a semi-opaque grey blue results.

234 Wide-firing base glaze

Feldspar	52
Whiting	18
Zinc oxide	10
Dolomite	5
China clay	10
Quartz	5

A wide-firing base glaze. In oxidation a smooth opaque white glaze develops, more speckled at 1260°C (2300°F). In reduction a clear shiny glaze. At 1200°C (2192°F) good results on RS (mottled white), YS (speckled matt), IS (pale green), BS (speckled blue grey) and GS (green grey). At 1260°C (2300°F) a blue orange white over RS in oxidation. In reduction rich iron (YS), blue black (BS).

Additions

(*a*) With copper oxide 1%, a green black speckle develops at 1200°C (2192°F), more runny at 1260°C (2300°F); pink in reduction.

(*b*) With iron oxide 4%, a speckled ochre in oxidation at 1200°–1260°C (2192°–2300°F), a rich green in reduction.

(*c*) With crocus martis, an orange ochre develops at 1200°–1260°C (2192°–2300°F). A rich dark green in reduction.

(*d*) With zirconium silicate 7%, a smooth matt white in oxidation, pale shiny blue in reduction.

(*e*) With tin oxide 4%, a delicate orange speckle develops in the matt white glaze in oxidation. In reduction a delicate pale shiny blue.

(*f*) With chrome oxide 1%, a pale matt beige develops in oxidation. A speckled shiny green in reduction.

(*g*) With nickel oxide 3%, a cream yellow develops.

(*h*) With copper carbonate 1%, a rich blue results.

1200°–1260°C (2192°–2300°F)

235 Semi-opaque crackle glaze

Feldspar	60
Whiting	10
China clay	5
Quartz	25

A bluish tint in reduction, this glaze crackles when thickly applied. 1220°–1260°C (2228°–2300°F)

236 Crystalline base glaze

Feldspar	50
Fluorspar	7
Flint	10
Zinc oxide	25
China clay	8

At 1200°C (2192°F) this glaze is a smooth satin matt giving soft greens over GS, electric blue over BS, yellow cream over RS. At 1260°C (2300°F) in oxidation frosty white crystalline formations develop over BS; these are blue black, creamy yellow over IS. In reduction no crystals form and the glaze is a smooth semi-transparent.

Additions

(*a*) With copper oxide 1%, pale green crystals develop in mid-green background on stoneware in oxidation, a smooth soft green at 1200°C (2192°F).

(*b*) With cobalt oxide 0.5%, electric blue crystalline textures develop, smooth at 1200°C (2192°F) in oxidation.

(*c*) With nickel oxide 1.5%, dark blue green crystalline formations result, more smooth in oxidation.

(*d*) With chrome oxide 1%, pale matt pinky brown glaze develops at 1200°C (2192°F) and 1260°C (2300°F) in oxidation (opaque green in reduction).

237 A dry base glaze

Feldspar	15
Nepheline syenite	5
Whiting	26
Calcium borate frit (P2254) (Colemanite)	3
China clay	51

A dry base glaze in which, with the addition of small amounts of oxides, matt muted colours develop. 1220°–1260°C (2228°–2300°F)

Additions

(*a*) With vanadium pentoxide 4% and cobalt carbonate 0.75%, gives a sea green.
(*b*) With vanadium pentoxide 4% and copper carbonate 2%, a speckled cream black.
(*c*) With vanadium pentoxide 2% and cobalt carbonate 0.75%, a soft medium blue.

238 A base reactive wood ash glaze

Wood ash	40
Soda feldspar	56
Bentonite	4

A semi-shiny glaze, more matt at lower temperatures. Blue black over BS; dark green over GS; ochre brown over IS; creamy white over RS in oxidation at 1260°C (2300°F). Rich tenmoku iron effects over YS in reduction.

Additions

(*a*) With rutile 3% and cobalt carbonate 0.5%, gives frosty blue at 1220°C (2228°F), more shiny at 1260°C (2300°F).
(*b*) With iron oxide 4%, an orange brown at 1220°C (2228°F), a matt ochre at 1260°C (2300°F), in reduction a shiny dark green.
(*c*) With iron oxide 8%, a red brown in oxidation at 1260°C (2300°F), a mottled red ochre in reduction.

239 Attractive base glaze

Soda feldspar	40
Whiting	15
Zinc oxide	11
Flint	26
China clay	8

A wide-range smooth clear craze-free transparent glaze in oxidation and reduction. Mottled blue black in oxidation over RS.

Additions

(*a*) With copper oxide 2%, a speckled mid-green develops at 1220°C (2228°F), slightly paler at 1260°C (2300°F). A pale pink in reduction.

(*b*) With iron oxide 2%, pale honey in oxidation, lovat green celadon in reduction.

(*c*) With iron oxide 5%, dark honey browns in oxidation, dark celadons in reduction.

(*d*) With nickel oxide 1%, and cobalt carbonate 0.5%, a blue purple glaze develops in oxidation, slightly paler in reduction.

(*e*) With chrome oxide 0.5% and cobalt oxide 0.5%, a mid-blue develops, more aquamarine in reduction.

240 Clear pale honey

Feldspar	35
Petalite	5
Barium carbonate	8
Calcium borate frit (P2954) (Colemanite)	15
Alkaline frit (P2962)	20
Fremington clay (Albany slip)	17

A clear pale honey-coloured glaze on porcelain, slightly more matt on stoneware. At 1260°C (2300°F) attractive tenmoku effect on IS.

Additions

(*a*) With iron oxide 5%, a dark olive on porcelain, dark brown on stoneware at 1200°C (2192°F). At 1260°C (2300°F) a smooth tenmoku on stoneware, more shiny on porcelain.

(*b*) With copper oxide 1.5%, attractive pale green on porcelain, an orange green on stoneware.

(*c*) With cobalt oxide 1%, rich dark blue black on porcelain, much darker on stoneware.

4. Decorative, crystalline and textural glazes

241 Smooth matt glaze decorative

Barium carbonate	15
Whiting	5
Zinc oxide	10
Feldspar	55
China clay	5
Flint	10

A smooth matt opaque glaze. Soft colours over slips at 1200°C (2192°F), more dramatic and intense at 1260°C (2300°F). Over RS, soft blue white at 1200°C (2192°F), blue black at 1260°C (2300°F).

Additions

(*a*) With nickel oxide 1.5%, a soft air-force blue with darker crystals; at higher temperatures the base is more khaki.

(*b*) With nickel oxide 1.5% and cobalt carbonate 0.5%, darker blue greys develop.

242 A reactive decorative glaze

Lithium carbonate	3
Barium carbonate	40
Zinc oxide	12
Nepheline syenite	25
Flint	16
Bentonite	4

A dry matt glaze giving soft mottled effects. Best when used with colouring oxides.

Additions

(*a*) With nickel oxide 1.5%, bright pink develops, more muted at 1260°C (2300°F).

(*b*) With nickel oxide 1.5% and cobalt oxide 0.5%, a mottled purple blue develops, richer at 1200°C (2192°F).

(*c*) With copper oxide 2%, a bright light turquoise results, most mottled at 1260°C (2300°F).

243 A reactive matt glaze (oxidation)

Soda feldspar	39
Zinc oxide	18
Barium carbonate	28
Flint	10
China clay	5

A smooth matt glaze with good rich results over slips at lower temperatures: soft green (GS), cream grey (RS), blue black (BS).

Additions

(*a*) With nickel oxide 1.5%, a purple mottled pink glaze develops in oxidation, more runny at higher temperatures.

(*b*) With nickel oxide 1.5% and cobalt carbonate 0.5%, purplish blue pink glaze develops.

(*c*) With chrome oxide 0.5%, a mottled pale cream brown develops at 1260°C (2300°F) on porcelain, slightly darker at lower temperatures.

244 A matt decorative reactive glaze

Barium carbonate	40
Soda feldspar	33
Zinc oxide	9.5
Lithium carbonate	1.5
China clay	11
Flint	5

A dry matt glaze base. If applied thinly over the slips, gives rich surfaces in oxidation, bubbles if applied too thickly.

Additions

(*a*) With nickel oxide 1.5%, bright pinks with pale blue crystal formations develop in oxidation, more pink at lower temperatures. Purple in reduction.

(*b*) With nickel oxide 1% and cobalt oxide 0.5%, purplish pink develops in oxidation, more blue in reduction.

245 Reactive pink white glaze

Barium carbonate	23
Nepheline syenite	45
Whiting	12
Dolomite	4
Titanium dioxide	4
Flint	5
China clay	7

A matt glaze which responds interestingly over slips and with oxide additions, in oxidation and reduction over a wide range of temperatures. Smooth cream pink over porcelain, much drier over stoneware.

Additions

(*a*) With copper oxide 1.5%, gives a pewter black in oxidation, a delicate mottled grey in reduction.

(*b*) With cobalt oxide 0.5%, delicate blue pink matt surfaces; result in reduction and on porcelain in oxidation: more green on stoneware.

(*c*) With chrome oxide 0.5% and copper oxide 1%, a purple green variation result in oxidation and reduction.

246 Decorative textured glaze

Alkaline frit (P2962)	40
Flint	30
China clay	30

A smooth semi-opaque white glaze at the low range of temperature; a more lava texture develops at higher temperatures. 1200°–1250°C (2192°–2282°F)

Addition

(*a*) With copper oxide 4%, a blue black develops on stoneware, a darker green on porcelain.

247 A crystalline base (oxidation)

Alkaline frit (P2962)	58
Zinc oxide	23
Flint	17
Bentonite	2

A crystalline base glaze which has a tendency to run, but a variety of crystals can be obtained in this recipe. By itself white needle-like crystals result.

Additions

(*a*) With chrome oxide 1%, a pale tan colour base with tan-coloured crystal markings.

(*b*) With nickel oxide 1.5%, gives a transparent brown with bright electric blue crystal markings.

248 Crystalline base

Zinc oxide	26
Feldspar	37
Whiting	13
Flint	18
China clay	6

A crystalline base glaze; smooth and opaque at 1200°C (2192°F), clear with white crystals at higher temperatures, 1260°C (2300°F).

249 A crystal-forming glaze

Feldspar	10
Whiting	5
Zinc oxide	20
Lithium carbonate	8
China clay	20
Flint	37

A matt glaze which on stoneware, and at higher temperatures, gives a white crystalline clear base; grey green mottled effect over RS.

Addition

(*a*) With chrome oxide 1%, an opaque pink brown glaze results.

250 Crystalline base glaze

Alkaline frit (P2962)	45
Zinc oxide	25
China clay	10
Flint	20
+ Titanium dioxide	6

A crystalline base glaze which gives white needle-like crystals. The tendency to run needs careful attention. In reduction a bright opalescent blue develops. 1200°–1250°C (2192°–2282°F)

251 Green red glaze

Borax frit (P2957)	10
Soda feldspar	40
Whiting	15
Zinc oxide	3
Quartz	27
China clay	5
+ Silicon carbide	0.5
Copper carbonate	2
Tin oxide	1

A bright green glaze; in reduction delicate red markings develop.

252 Black bronze effect glaze

China clay	33
Manganese oxide	33
Copper oxide	33

A smooth matt black with bronze markings over a wide temperature range.

253 Broken wood ash glaze (oxidation)

Wood ash	40
Feldspar	32
Whiting	10
China clay	18

A matt broken pale green ochre glaze, particularly attractive on stoneware over a wide temperature range.

Addition

(*a*) With iron oxide 2%, a more interesting speckled surface develops; too runny in reduction.

254 Runny ash glaze

Wood ash	50
Dolomite	23
Talc	3
China clay	15
Flint	9

A broken pale green mottled ash glaze over a wide temperature range.

Addition

(*a*) With iron oxide 2%, a more green brown glaze.

255 A wide firing ash glaze

Wood ash	45
Barium carbonate	10
Fremington clay (Albany slip)	45

A pale yellow mottled ash glaze, less broken at 1200°C (2192°F), in oxidation. A dark ochre green in reduction.

Addition

(*a*) With cobalt oxide 1%, a mottled dark ink blue on porcelain in reduction; a more matt mottled iron blue on porcelain in oxidation at 1260°C (2300°F). A green ochre at 1200°C (2192°F).

256 Blue pink matt

Soda feldspar	40
Whiting	15
Zinc oxide	5
Barium carbonate	5
Talc	35
+ Cobalt carbonate	1.5

A pinky blue matt glaze at 1200°C (2192°F), more blue and runny at 1260°C (2300°F) in oxidation. A matt blue brown in reduction.

1260°C (2300°F) Orton cone 8

1. Bright, clear, opaque and white glazes

257 Clear bright glaze

Soda feldspar	44
Whiting	15
Flint	24
Calcium borate frit (P2954) (Colemanite)	10
China clay	7

A clear, smooth basic glaze.

258 Good clear base glaze

Calcium borate frit (P2954) (Colemanite)	5
Dolomite	24
Feldspar	22
Ball clay	25
Flint	24

A good clear base glaze.

259 Good clear base

Calcium borate frit (P2954) (Colemanite)	5
Dolomite	25
Nepheline syenite	20
Ball clay	25
Flint	25

A reliable clear glaze; creamy in oxidation, slightly greyer in reduction. Over IS a rich black iron tenmoku in oxidation; over YS in reduction a green brown black.

260 Clear transparent

Feldspar	40
Whiting	18
China clay	13
Flint	29

A clear transparent glaze, slightly milky on stoneware. Attractive grey and black mottled effect on IS.

261 Clear

Feldspar	30
Whiting	20
China clay	20
Flint	30

A basic clear glaze, smooth and bright, brown and green mottle over YS.

262 Clear bright glaze

Feldspar	15
Whiting	23
China clay	25
Flint	37

A good basic clear glaze; brown green mottle over YS.

263 Clear, craze-free transparent

Alkaline frit (P2962)	10
Dolomite	25
Feldspar	20
Ball clay	25
Flint	20

A smooth craze-free transparent glaze. Rich black brown and white mottled over IS, black brown over YS.

264 Good clear, non-crazed clear

Calcium borate frit (P2954) (Colemanite)	5
Dolomite	25
Spodumene	20
Ball clay	25
Flint	25

A clear slightly green glaze in reduction; a pale cream in reduction.

265 Clear (reduction)

Soda feldspar	80
Whiting	10
Zinc oxide	5
China clay	5

A clear, semi-opaque glaze in reduction; in oxidation a frosty more opaque glaze, a pale blue grey over RS. In reduction grey blue (RS), blue black (BS).

266 Clear, slightly crackle glaze

Dolomite	20
Feldspar	63
China clay	12
Flint	5

A clear, semi-crackle glaze in oxidation, more blue grey in reduction.

267 Smooth semi-clear reduction

Feldspar	30
Whiting	20
Barium carbonate	7
China clay	8
Flint	35

A strong pale blue white in reduction; stiff in oxidation. Good smooth results over RS, IS, BS and YS. Pink flashing over GS.

268 Clear transparent glaze

Feldspar	30
Calcium borate frit (P2954) (Colemanite)	12
Whiting	10
Barium carbonate	10
Dolomite	3
Quartz	30
China clay	5

Good basic clear transparent glaze in oxidation and reduction on porcelain and stoneware; similar results in oxidation and stoneware. Over BS attractive blue grey; on GS, good attractive iron spots; YS, good eggshell speckle.

269 Smooth clear glaze (reduction)

Cornish (Cornwall) stone	20
Feldspar	10
Whiting	25
Quartz	20
China clay	25

A smooth clear glaze, pale blue in reduction.

Addition

(*a*) With iron oxide 1.5%, a medium green celadon glaze in reduction.

270 Pale blue porcelain (reduction)

Nepheline syenite	10
Cornish (Cornwall) stone	40
Whiting	22
Flint	5
China clay	23

A smooth semi-matt pale blue porcelain glaze (reduction). An opaque white porcelain glaze in oxidation.

271 A semi-clear base glaze

Feldspar	55
Dolomite	11
Alkaline frit (P2962)	4
Whiting	6
Flint	21
Bentonite	3

A smooth semi-clear base glaze in oxidation and reduction.

Additions

(*a*) With iron oxide 2%, pale celadon in reduction, creamy in reduction.

(*b*) With iron oxide 5%, dark celadon, green in reduction, and oxidation on stoneware.

(*c*) With iron oxide 8%, rich tenmoku on stoneware in oxidation and reduction.

272 Smooth semi-clear glaze

Feldspar	35
Whiting	20
Dolomite	3
Ball clay	24
Flint	18

A smooth semi-clear glaze, more speckled in reduction.

Addition

(*a*) With zircon 10%, a white opaque glaze results.

273 Smooth bright crackle

Feldspar	80
Whiting	5
Quartz	15

A stiff smooth bright crackle glaze, blue tint in reduction.

274 Clear, slightly crackled glaze

Calcium borate frit (P2954) (Colemanite)	2
Feldspar	48
Talc	5
Whiting	20
Quartz	15
China clay	10

A slightly runny clear glaze in oxidation, with blue grey colour in reduction. Excellent iron greens over YS in reduction.

275 Smooth semi-clear glaze

Cornish (Cornwall) stone	58
Whiting	20
Talc	5
Bone ash	3
China clay	13

A smooth semi-opaque white glaze in oxidation, more shiny in reduction. In oxidation, an ochre red green over IS; a smooth creamy white over RS; a blue black over BS. In reduction dark iron red green over YS.

276 Slightly milky transparent

Feldspar	70
Whiting	14
Flint	13
Bentonite	3

A clear glaze with a tendency to crackle. Dark blue with oil spot effect over BS, brown green mottle over IS.

277 Clear slightly crackled glaze

Feldspar	70
Whiting	15
Dolomite	5
China clay	7
Quartz	3

A clear slightly crackled glaze, shiny in reduction, drier in oxidation.

278 Semi-clear reduction

Feldspar	38
China clay	10
Dolomite	16
Whiting	7
Flint	29

A semi-clear, slightly frosty glaze in reduction. Good results over YS, BS, IS and RS. Do not apply too thickly.

279 A frosty clear glaze

Bone ash	5
Soda feldspar	55
Whiting	17
Flint	23

A clear, slightly frosty glaze in oxidation, a frosty blue grey in reduction. A red green over IS, a blue grey BS in oxidation. In reduction an iron brown green over IS; a blue grey over BS; a rich brown black over YS.

280 Clear, slightly crackle glaze

Whiting	5
Soda feldspar	60
Wollastonite	25
Bone ash	5
China clay	5

A clear, slightly crackled colourless glaze in oxidation, more blue white in reduction. Red grey green (YS), matt blue grey (BS), in oxidation. In reduction, brown blue (IS), iron red (YS).

281 A muted semi-clear glaze

Dolomite	20
Feldspar	63
Ball clay	12
Flint	5

A slightly crackled semi-clear glaze in oxidation, a frosty blue grey in reduction.

282 Smooth speckle white

Cornish (Cornwall) stone	50
Whiting	24
China clay	24
Bone ash	2

Semi-opaque satin white in oxidation, speckled on stoneware. Blue white in reduction, an attractive semi-matt on porcelain. Excellent colour response from YS (red green), IS (brown green) and BS (blue black) in oxidation. In reduction YS (green grey and red), BS (dark blue black) and IS (blue grey and red).

Addition

(*a*) With copper carbonate 1% and rutile 2%, a deep red results.

283 Satin white

Nepheline syenite	40
Cornish (Cornwall) stone	10
Whiting	5
Dolomite	25
China clay	20

A satin white fairly dry base glaze; smooth and white in oxidation, pale blue in reduction.

Additions

(*a*) With tin oxide 2%, gives more speckled orange coloured glaze in oxidation.

(*b*) With cobalt oxide 0.5% and rutile 2.5%, gives a pale blue grey in oxidation on stoneware.

284 Smooth satin cool white

Feldspar	30
Cornish (Cornwall) stone	20
Whiting	5
Dolomite	25
China clay	20

A smooth white in oxidation, a pale blue in reduction. Good iron colours over IS in oxidation.

Additions

(*a*) With tin oxide 1.5%, gives an orange speckle in oxidation.
(*b*) With cobalt oxide 0.5% and rutile 2.5%, smooth pale blue grey tones result.

285 Smooth matt satin white

Cornish (Cornwall) stone	50
Whiting	5
Dolomite	25
China clay	20

A smooth matt white satin glaze in oxidation, a pale blue in reduction. Good results over slips. In oxidation soft creamy tones over RS, GS, IS and BS. Dramatic mottles over YS. In reduction good dark response from YS, IS and BS.

Additions

(*a*) With cobalt oxide 0.5% and rutile 2.5%, gives soft pale grey blues in oxidation and reduction.
(*b*) With tin oxide 2%, enhances speckle orange effect in oxidation.

286 Semi-opaque orange white

Calcium borate frit (P2954) (Colemanite)	5
Dolomite	24
Spodumene	17
Feldspar	5
Ball clay	25
Flint	24
+ Tin oxide	5

An attractive milky orange semi-opaque glaze on stoneware in oxidation. In reduction a pale celadon results.

287 Smooth opaque glaze

Feldspar	35
Whiting	20
Talc	10
Flint	10
China clay	25

A smooth creamy white opaque on porcelain in oxidation, a pale blue in reduction.

Addition

(*a*) With titanium dioxide 5%, a rich mottled orange grey in reduction, a creamy white in oxidation.

288 Smooth well-fitting semi-opaque

Feldspar	45
Whiting	15
Talc	15
China clay	15
Flint	10

A smooth well-fitting semi-opaque glaze, slightly more matt in reduction.

289 Speckled white

Calcium borate frit (P2954) (Colemanite)	5
Dolomite	25
Feldspar	20
Ball clay	25
Flint	25
+ Tin oxide	5

A smooth white with an orange speckle on stoneware in oxidation. A pale celadon in reduction.

Addition

(*a*) With iron oxide 4%, an Indian red results in oxidation, an olive celadon in reduction.

290 Milky white speckle

Calcium borate frit (P2954) (Colemanite)	6
Nepheline syenite	19
Dolomite	25
Ball clay	25
Flint	25
+ Tin oxide	5

A smooth milky white glaze with attractive speckle in oxidation. In reduction a slightly milky celadon.

291 Smooth opaque white

Nepheline syenite	40
Petalite	6
Calcium borate frit (P2954) (Colemanite)	14
Flint	20
Ball clay	20
+ Tin oxide	4

A smooth opaque soft white with orange speckle.

292 Semi-opaque white

Feldspar	35
Dolomite	25
China clay	10
Quartz	30

A semi-opaque white matt.

293 Snowy white

Feldspar	32
Calcium borate frit (P2954) (Colemanite)	12
Whiting	10
Barium carbonate	10
Dolomite	4
Quartz	28
China clay	4
+ Tin oxide	6

A smooth clean snowy white.

294 Soft cream speckle

Borax frit (P2957)	22
Talc	22
Whiting	5
Petalite	10
Feldspar	10
Ball clay	20
Flint	11
+ Zirconium oxide	10

In electric kiln a soft pale grey with iron speckle. Do not apply thickly.

295 Satin matt creamy glaze

Feldspar	20
Dolomite	10
Whiting	15
China clay	30
Flint	25

Delicate pale blue in reduction, creamy in oxidation. Excellent results in reduction over BS (blue black), IS (brown grey), YS (brown green), RS (soft grey) and GS (copper pink).

296 Frosty opaque

Feldspar	40
Whiting	20
Talc	3
Calcium borate frit (P2954) (Colemanite)	2
China clay	5
Quartz	30

A semi-opaque frosty glaze: matt in oxidation, more shiny in reduction.

Addition

(*a*) With iron oxide 1%, a delicate lovat green develops in reduction, a pale honey in oxidation.

297 Smooth semi-opaque speckle glaze

Feldspar	38
Whiting	10
Dolomite	18
Flint	30
Bentonite	4

A smooth semi-opaque white glaze which develops an attractive speckle over stoneware. Slightly more matt in oxidation.

Addition

(*a*) With rutile 5% and cobalt oxide 0.5%, a powder blue glaze develops.

298 Soft opaque white

Feldspar	45
Petalite	18
Dolomite	16
Whiting	6
Flint	5
China clay	10
+ Tin oxide	5

A semi-opaque blue white with speckles in reduction and in oxidation on stoneware. On porcelain clear pale green in reduction, an opaque white in oxidation.

299 Smooth semi-opaque white

Nepheline syenite	40
Cornish (Cornwall) stone	22
Whiting	20
China clay	18

A smooth matt white glaze in reduction; in oxidation in the electric kiln the glaze is drier and more matt on the slightly textured surface on stoneware; smooth on porcelain.

Addition

(*a*) With tin oxide 3%, a slightly bluer, more opaque glaze in reduction; a more creamy pink on porcelain in the electric kiln. A drier smooth opaque white on porcelain at 1200°C (2192°F).

300 Opaque blue/white glaze

Nepheline syenite	25
Whiting	20
Feldspar	15
China clay	7
Flint	33
+ Zircon	9

A smooth speckled opaque white on stoneware, more milky on porcelain in reduction. In oxidation more opaque glaze.

301 Smooth cool opaque white

Nepheline syenite	15
Soda feldspar	35
Petalite	28
Alkaline frit (P2962)	10
China clay	12

A smooth semi-opaque cool white in reduction, a semi-clear crackle in oxidation.

Addition
(*a*) With tin oxide 3%, a more opaque glaze results.

302 Smooth matt

Zinc oxide	10
Feldspar	40
Dolomite	15
Barium carbonate	25
Ball clay	10

A smooth matt white glaze, breaking with soft iron speckle where thin.

Addition
(*a*) With zircon 15%, a dense white matt glaze results.

303 Smooth white matt

Feldspar	50
Whiting	20
China clay	20
Flint	10

A smooth white semi-matt glaze, more speckled in reduction.

304 Speckle matt glaze

Feldspar	30
Dolomite	30
Whiting	5
China clay	30
Flint	5
+ Tin oxide	3

A smooth white matt glaze with brown speckle on stoneware in reduction and oxidation. Smoother on porcelain.

Addition

(*a*) With red iron oxide 0.75%, the glaze is more creamy coloured.

305 Silky matt white

Feldspar	50
Barium carbonate	20
Flint	5
Whiting	13
China clay	12

A silky smooth matt glaze in oxidation, slightly speckled in reduction. Pale green black over GS, ochre mottle over IS in oxidation. In reduction iron green over IS.

306 Opaque white crackle (oxidation)

Feldspar	35
Quartz	40
Whiting	20
China clay	5

An opaque white crackle glaze when thickly applied in oxidation which takes stains well.

307 Semi-matt white

Nepheline syenite	40
Dolomite	22
Barium carbonate	16
Ball clay	10
Flint	12

A smooth grey white on stoneware and porcelain in reduction. In the electric kiln the glaze is matt white with speckles on stoneware, smoother on porcelain.

Addition

(*a*) With tin oxide 3%, the glaze is more speckled.

308 Semi-matt clear

Feldspar	42
Whiting	20
Flint	20
Talc	6
China clay	12

Attractive pale blue crackle glaze in reduction. Dull in oxidation unless 4% tin oxide is added, which gives good milky whites. In reduction the glaze is excellent over BS, IS, YS (red and brown) and GS (copper red).

309 Pale matt glaze

Cornish (Cornwall) stone	55
Whiting	25
Red clay	20

A dry matt speckle in oxidation, a soft heather green in reduction. Good colour response over slips; do not apply too thickly.

Addition

(*a*) With cobalt oxide 1.5%, dark blue black, drier in oxidation, more shiny in reduction.

310 Semi-matt smooth glaze, good with iron oxide

Cornish (Cornwall) stone	54
Whiting	24
China clay	22

Semi-matt glaze smooth on porcelain, dry on stoneware in oxidation. More glassy in reduction. Excellent iron speckle over YS. Matt white crystal glaze over RS in oxidation.

In oxidation iron with 2%, 5% and 8% oxide, moves from plate green to medium ochre, to rich dark yellow ochre. In reduction darker shades develop.

311 Semi-matt clear

Feldspar	55
Whiting	20
China clay	7
Flint	18

A semi-matt clear glaze with crackle if applied thickly.

312 Semi-matt clear

Whiting	12
Barium carbonate	12
Feldspar	33
China clay	15
Flint	28

A stiff glaze which needs 1280°C (2336°F) to mature. Good results over BS, IS and YS.

2. Speckle and coloured glazes

313 Smooth barium glaze

Nepheline syenite	62
Barium carbonate	24
Lithium carbonate	2
Flint	5
China clay	7

A smooth satin barium semi-opaque matt in reduction.

314 Smooth speckle white (reduction)

Feldspar	28
Talc	18
Whiting	12
China clay	16
Flint	26

A smooth white speckle opaque glaze in reduction.

315 Speckle titanium matt

Feldspar	48
Titanium dioxide	5
Zinc oxide	5
Whiting	21
China clay	21

A smooth matt speckle glaze on stoneware, whiter on porcelain, in both oxidation and reduction.

Addition

(*a*) With zircon 10%, a whiter more opaque glaze results.

316 Speckle semi-matt

Nepheline syenite	38
Cornish (Cornwall) stone	18
Whiting	20
Zinc oxide	6
China clay	18

A semi-matt speckle glaze on stoneware in reduction and oxidation.

Addition

(*a*) With tin oxide 3%, a more opaque speckle results.

317 Semi-matt grey blue

Cornish (Cornwall) stone	10
Feldspar	10
Whiting	20
China clay	20
Ball clay	20
Flint	20
+ Cobalt carbonate	0.5
Nickel oxide	1

A semi-matt grey blue glaze, darker in reduction.

318 Frosty ice-blue

Feldspar	40
Calcium borate frit (P2954) (Colemanite)	5
Zinc oxide	8
Dolomite	6
Talc	12
Flint	20
China clay	9
+ Cobalt oxide	0.5

In oxidation a frosty muted sea blue, more frosty when thick. A brighter blue in reduction.

319 Pale blue

Nepheline syenite	12
Feldspar	28
Whiting	31
Ball clay	29
+ Cobalt oxide	0.5
Rutile	7

A pale blue in oxidation, a more runny glaze in reduction.

320 Opaque blue

Feldspar	56
Dolomite	20
Red clay	24
+ Cobalt oxide	1

A dark midnight blue with iron speckles in reduction; a dark grey blue in oxidation.

321 Smooth blue matt

Whiting	7
Mixed wood ash	30
Soda feldspar	23
Potash feldspar	10
China clay	25
Red clay	5
+ Cobalt oxide	1

A blue ochre speckled in oxidation, a darker blue in reduction. A dry blue grey speckle at 1200°C (2192°F).

322 Midnight blue glaze

Cornish (Cornwall) stone	55
Whiting	25
China clay	15
Ball clay	5
+ Cobalt carbonate	0.5
Nickel oxide	0.5

A smooth dark rich midnight blue glaze.

323 Rich turquoise

Feldspar	51
Barium carbonate	19
Flint	5
Whiting	14
China clay	11
+ Copper oxide	1.5

A smooth rich turquoise with black crystal formations in oxidation; a shiny pink green mottle in reduction.

324 Turquoise blue (oxidation)

Nepheline syenite	60
Barium carbonate	25
Lithium carbonate	2
Flint	4
China clay	7
+ Copper oxide	1.5

A bright turquoise blue on porcelain in oxidation, more muted on stoneware.

325 Smooth matt pale green porcelain

Calcium borate frit (P2954) (Colemanite)	5
Nepheline syenite	42
Whiting	17
Bone ash	7
Talc	5
China clay	12
Flint	12
+ Yellow iron ochre	0.5
Copper carbonate	0.25

A soft green in oxidation on porcelain, a green brown on stoneware. In reduction, particularly beautiful pink and green semi-matt glaze.

326 Mid-green glaze

Barium carbonate	19
Whiting	14
Feldspar	50
Flint	6
China clay	11
+ Cobalt oxide	0.5
Nickel oxide	

A muted mid-green-coloured glaze.

327 Pale green

Feldspar	68
Whiting	16
Dolomite	6
China clay	6
Quartz	4
+ Copper carbonate	2

Smooth pale greens in oxidation; pale pink greys in reduction firings.

328 Pale blue grey (reduction)

Barium carbonate	25
Lithium carbonate	2
Feldspar	60
Flint	4
China clay	7

A pale semi-matt blue grey in reduction; a drier cream white in oxidation.

329 Delicate blue white semi-matt (reduction)

Feldspar	35
Dolomite	5
Whiting	20
Flint	15
China clay	25

Dull in oxidation; excellent in reduction on stoneware and porcelain. Sensitive to copper oxide and gives pink flashing. Good results over BS, YS, IS and RS in reduction.

330 Chun type glaze

Feldspar	40
Whiting	20
Talc	4
Calcium borate frit (P2954) (Colemanite)	2
China clay	5
Flint	29
+ Titanium dioxide	2

An opaque chun type glaze in oxidation; a smoother result in reduction.

331 Ying ching effect, pale blue glaze

Alkaline frit (P2962)	20
Zinc oxide	20
Whiting	20
Flint	36
Bentonite	4

A pale bright opalescent blue in reduction; more muted and chun type in oxidation. At lower temperatures a more crystalline glaze develops. Do not apply too thickly.

Addition

(*a*) With titanium oxide 3% and rutile 5%, soft pink crystals can develop in a white base glaze.

332 Pale blue carbon trap glaze

Calcium borate frit (P2254) (Colemanite)	4
Whiting	18
Talc	6
Feldspar	42
Flint	27
Bentonite	3

A bright but delicate blue in reduction on stoneware, in reduction and in the electric kiln.

Addition

(*a*) With tin oxide 1%, copper carbonate 1% and silicon carbide 0.5%, a blue mauve develops in reduction and oxidation, on stoneware and porcelain.

333 A dark navy blue

Feldspar	43
Whiting	25
Flint	20
China clay	12
+ Cobalt oxide	1.5
Iron oxide	1

A smooth dark navy blue both in oxidation and reduction.

334 Soft lovat blue

Whiting	25
Flint	40
China clay	20
Ball clay	15

A smooth semi-matt lovat blue grey in oxidation and reduction.

335 Blue grey glaze

Cornish (Cornwall) stone	65
Whiting	12
China clay	15
Quartz	8
+ Cobalt oxide	0.5
Manganese dioxide	2
Iron oxide	1

A smooth opaque blue grey glaze.

336 Copper red glaze

Zinc oxide	2
Soda feldspar	30
Borax frit (P2257)	5
Alkaline frit (P2962)	24
Whiting	6
China clay	6
Flint	27
+ Tin oxide	2
Copper carbonate	0.5
Silicon carbide	0.75

The base glaze is a clear crackle. With the additions listed, a rich bright red develops in reduction on stoneware and porcelain. Do not overfire. In the electric kiln a dark grey red glaze develops.

Addition

(a) With red iron oxide 1%, the red is more muted in reduction, and more celadon green with red markings on porcelain in the electric kiln.

337 Copper red glaze

Barium carbonate	28
Feldspar	38
Petalite	16
China clay	8
Flint	10
+ Copper cabonate	1.5

A rich copper red glaze in reduction. In oxidation at lower temperatures a soft green turquoise develops.

338 Dusky pink (oxidation)

Feldspar	42
Whiting	17
Talc	2
Zinc oxide	5
Quartz	26
China clay	8
+ Silicon carbide	1
Copper carbonate	0.5

A dusky pink grey glaze.

339 Frosty pink

Soda feldspar	45
Whiting	14
Flint	24
Calcium borate frit (P2254) (Colemanite)	10
China clay	7
+ Tin oxide	2
Copper carbonate	0.5
Silicon carbide	1

A frosty pink red in oxidation; a mottled pink grey in reduction.

340 Bright pink

Soda feldspar	40
Alkaline frit (P2262)	30
Whiting	10
China clay	15
Quartz	5
+ Tin oxide	2
Copper carbonate	0.5
Silicon carbide	1

A bright pink in reduction, a darker red in oxidation.

341 Dark blue

Feldspar	56
Whiting	24
Red clay	20
+ Cobalt oxide	1.5

A smooth dark blue glaze in oxidation and reduction.

342 Indian red

Nepheline syenite	22
Calcium borate frit (P2954) (Colemanite)	5
Dolomite	24
Ball clay	24
Flint	25
+ Tin oxide	3
Iron oxide	3

A smooth bright Indian red in oxidation; in reduction a dark attractive speckled celadon glaze.

343 Pale celadon grey

Feldspar	40
Cornish (Cornwall) stone	10
Zinc oxide	3
Whiting	17
China clay	11
Flint	19
+ Iron oxide	2

A bright green grey celadon in reduction; a pale honey in oxidation.

344 Pale blue green celadon 1260°–1280°C (2300°–2336°F)

Feldspar	60
Whiting	10
China clay	5
Flint	25
+ Iron oxide	2

(*a*) A smooth blue green celadon on stoneware and porcelain in reduction. 7% iron oxide with results in a shiny tenmoku.

345 Celadon (reduction)

Dolomite	20
Feldspar	63
Red clay	12
Flint	5

A smooth muted celadon glaze in reduction; a pale honey in oxidation.

346 Celadon (reduction)

Feldspar	55
Dolomite	20
Red clay	25

A pale lovat green celadon in reduction; a pale honey in oxidation.

Addition

(*a*) With zirconium silicate 10%, the glaze takes on a slightly more opaque smooth quality.

347 Pale celadon 1260°–1280°C (2300°–2336°F)

Soda feldspar	42
Flint	25
Whiting	18
China clay	15
+ Iron oxide	2
Silicon carbide (fine)	0.75

A smooth pale celadon glaze in oxidation.

348 Pale matt celadon blue (reduction)

Feldspar	38
Cornish (Cornwall) stone	18
Whiting	20
Zinc oxide	6
China clay	18

An attractive smooth pale blue celadon semi-matt glaze in reduction. An opaque white in oxidation.

349 Pale blue green clear (reduction)

Feldspar	22
Cornish (Cornwall) stone	11
Whiting	28
China clay	22
Flint	17
+ Iron oxide	1

A smooth soft clear celadon glaze in reduction. Without the iron oxide the glaze is a soft pale blue.

350 Matt brown orange glaze

Nepheline syenite	65
Whiting	10
Bone ash	3
China clay	7
Flint	15
+ Iron oxide	6

A matt brown orange yellow glaze in oxidation; a more sticky-looking tenmoku in reduction.

351 Brown mottle

Feldspar	35
Whiting	12
Barium carbonate	23
China clay	15
Flint	15

A smooth semi-matt glaze with rich brown iron spot texture over IS in oxidation and reduction.

352 Olive brown

Cornish (Cornwall) stone	53
Whiting	24
Red clay	23
+ Iron oxide	5

A reddish olive green in oxidation; more olive brown in reduction.

353 Mottled orange brown (oxidation)

Calcium borate frit (P2954) (Colemanite)	5
Dolomite	21
Spodumene	19
Ball clay	24
Flint	26
+ Tin oxide	4
Iron oxide	4

A rich smooth mottled orange brown in oxidation; a dark olive in reduction.

354 Mottled hare's fur black

Feldspar	53
Dolomite	21
Red clay	26
+ Iron oxide	5

A mattish hare's fur in oxidation; a smooth mottled black brown in reduction.

355 Mottled brown glaze

Feldspar	67
Whiting	16
Dolomite	6
China clay	7
Flint	4
+Iron oxide	8

A smooth interesting mottled brown green in oxidation; a more shiny glaze in reduction.

356 Orange brown

Feldspar	36
Whiting	21
Talc	9
Flint	10
China clay	24
+ Rutile	25

A mid-orange brown glaze in oxidation and reduction.

357 Matt red brown

Feldspar	60
Whiting	20
China clay	10
Quartz	10
+ Iron oxide	8

A semi-matt red brown in oxidation, lighter in colour on porcelain, more shiny red brown in reduction.

358 Brown orange glaze

Feldspar	50
Whiting	5
Dolomite	5
Bone ash	15
China clay	5
Flint	20
+ Iron oxide	8

An opaque brown glaze with black mottled markings in oxidation and reduction.

359 Dark matt red brown

Cornish (Cornwall) stone	18
Feldspar	12
Whiting	25
Quartz	21
China clay	24
+ Iron oxide	8

A matt, mottled red brown glaze.

360 A medium brown speckle matt

Feldspar	40
Dolomite	20
Red clay	40

A smooth medium brown speckle matt glaze in oxidation; more shiny in reduction.

361 Red brown

Feldspar	50
Petalite	10
Bone ash	12
Dolomite	7
Calcium borate frit (P2954) (Colemanite)	4
China clay	6
Flint	11
+ Iron oxide	5

In oxidation a smooth red brown speckled glaze, brighter on stoneware.

Addition

(*a*) With iron oxide 4%, a red orange glaze develops.

362 A semi-matt mottled black brown

Feldspar	50
Whiting	20
China clay	15
Flint	15
+ Crocus martis	8

An attractive mottled brown black glaze, more matt in oxidation.

363 A rich shiny dark olive

Feldspar	45
Whiting	20
China clay	10
Flint	25
+ Iron oxide	9

A smooth dark olive brown glaze. More broken in reduction.

364 Brown chun 1260°–1280°C

Talc	5
Whiting	15
Feldspar	35
Ball clay	10
China clay	10
Flint	25
+ Iron oxide	3
Titanium oxide	4

A shiny brown glaze with chun blues.

365 Pale iron speckle glaze

Feldspar	40
Dolomite	15
Whiting	10
Red clay	10
China clay	20
Flint	5

An attractive grey iron speckle glaze in reduction, smooth and matt, gives a drier surface in oxidation. Excellent iron response in oxidation for GS and IS. In reduction good over BS.

366 Speckle tenmoku

Feldspar	60
Whiting	8
China clay	5
Flint	27
+ Iron oxide	8

A rich black brown tenmoku with speckle in reduction on stoneware and porcelain. In oxidation a more muted dark brown with oil spot markings when thickly applied.

367 Dark tenmoku

Feldspar	34
Flint	40
Whiting	17
China clay	9
+ Iron oxide	11

A smooth dark tenmoku which develops subtle browns where applied more thinly.

368 Tenmoku

Feldspar	65
Whiting	12
China clay	8
Flint	15
+ Crocus martis	8

A good black breaking brown in reduction, slightly more muted in oxidation.

369 Tenmoku (reduction)

Whiting	10
Feldspar	60
Fremington clay	30
(Albany clay)	10
+ Iron oxide	7

In reduction a good smooth satin black brown over stoneware and porcelain. In oxidation a satin matt subdued glaze at 1260°C (2300°F), more shiny and broken at 1280°C (2336°F).

370 Semi-matt tenmoku

Soda feldspar	50
Whiting	8
Dolomite	7
Bone ash	14
Flint	16
China clay	5

A semi-shiny black brown in oxidation; more shiny in reduction.

371 Oil spot glaze

Nepheline syenite	70
Alkaline frit (P2962)	10
Yellow ochre	20
+ Bentonite	3

A smooth bright black brown glaze with typical oil spot markings in oxidation. A smooth lustrous brown in reduction.

Addition

(*a*) With iron oxide 5%, a darker oil spot glaze results.

372 Rich dark brown oil spot

Nepheline syenite	75
Cornish (Cornwall) stone	11
Iron oxide	10
Bentonite	4

A rich black brown with oil spot marking if thickly applied in the electric kiln on stoneware and porcelain. A more burnt brown in reduction.

373 Bright black brown

Feldspar	50
Flint	15
China clay	15
Flint	20
+ Manganese carbonate	4
Iron oxide	3
Cobalt oxide	1

A smooth bright black brown glaze.

3. Base glazes

374 Clear, smooth glaze, good for colour additions

Feldspar	30
Whiting	10
Dolomite	20
China clay	15
Quartz	25

A basic clear glaze in oxidation and reduction. In oxidation excellent green brown results over GS. Interesting blue brown mottling over RS. In reduction good results over BS and IS.

Additions

(*a*) With copper oxide 3%, speckled green (oxidation).

(*b*) With cobalt oxide 0.5%, speckled inky blue (oxidation).

(*c*) With iron oxide 5%, mottled black brown (oxidation), dark olive green (reduction).

375 Stiff semi-clear glaze base

Cornish (Cornwall) stone	35
Nepheline syenite	45
Dolomite	10
China clay	10

Apply thinly. A semi-opaque sparkled glaze over stoneware in reduction, a more matt surface in reduction. Good over BS (dark blue with iron speckle) and YS (medium brown black).

Additions

(*a*) With copper oxide 1%, a rich *sang de boeuf* in reduction; in oxidation matt green with pink spots on porcelain.

(*b*) With tin oxide 3%, a brighter glaze results in reduction; an opaque white on porcelain in oxidation.

376 Clear glaze with slight crackle, good for colour

Feldspar	60
Whiting	15
Dolomite	5
China clay	8
Quartz	12

A clear, smooth glaze with slight crackle, more blue in reduction.

Additions

(*a*) With copper carbonate 2%, a pale clear green in oxidation, a pink in reduction. At 1220°C (2228°F) in oxidation a semi-matt opaque green.

(*b*) With cobalt carbonate 1%, rich deep midnight blues.

(*c*) With iron oxide 2%, a shiny mid-green celadon in reduction, a muted honey in oxidation.

377 Clear, semi-shiny glaze, good for iron additions

Feldspar	38
Whiting	18
China clay	14
Flint	30

Clear semi-shine in oxidation, in reduction stiffish with slight craze. Dark blue black over BS in oxidation and reduction. Interesting iron brown and yellow speckle over IS.

Excellent base for additions of iron oxide, gives red browns in oxidation (i.e. 5%, 8%), and with 8% iron oxide tenmoku on stoneware in reduction.

378 Slightly frosty clear base glaze

Feldspar	30
Whiting	12
Dolomite	16
China clay	17
Quartz	25

A pale blue grey slightly frosty glaze in reduction, creamy in oxidation. Iron red tenmoku over YS in reduction.

Additions

(*a*) With copper oxide 4%, an attractive peach bloom develops in reduction: pink red when thick, mottled green when thinner. Medium dark green in oxidation.

(*b*) With iron oxide 8%, a mattish red brown develops in oxidation, more shiny in reduction.

379 Smooth clear base glaze

Feldspar	50
Whiting	20
China clay	15
Flint	15

A smooth clear base glaze.

Additions

(*a*) With iron oxide 8%, a rich dark brown red results on stoneware, more ochre on porcelain in oxidation and reduction.

(*b*) With copper oxide 1.5%, rutile 3% and iron oxide 2%, a green brown glaze breaking darker brown.

380 Good iron base (reduction)

Feldspar	70
Whiting	10
China clay	10
Flint	10

Base glaze in reduction a smooth pale blue on porcelain, speckle on stoneware. Good smooth iron grey effects over IS and YS.

Additions (reduction)

(*a*) With iron oxide 3%, green celadon.
(*b*) With iron oxide 6%, bright tenmoku.
(*c*) With iron oxide 9%, smooth dark red brown.

381 Satin opaque white, excellent with iron additions

Cornish (Cornwall) stone	35
Feldspar	45
Whiting	10
China clay	10

A crackled satin glaze in oxidation and reduction. Will fire well to 1280°C (2336°F).

Additions

(*a*) With iron oxide 2%, a delicate pale green celadon in reduction.
(*b*) With iron oxide 8%, a rich semi-matt black brown in reduction, a more matt result in oxidation.

382 Clear base glaze for iron oxide

Feldspar	25
Whiting	25
China clay	25
Quartz	25

The base glaze gives good results over IS and YS. A good blue grey base in reduction, pale cream in oxidation.

Additions

(*a*) With iron oxide 2%, gives pale green in reduction, pale olive in oxidation.

(*b*) With iron oxide 5%, gives dark olive green in reduction, matt medium green brown in oxidation.

(*c*) With iron oxide 8%, gives rich red brown in reduction, and matt red brown in oxidation.

383 Iron base glaze 1260°–1280°C (2300–2336°F)

Cornish (Cornwall) stone	65
Whiting	12
China clay	8
Flint	15

A smooth semi-opaque high-firing glaze 1280°C (2336°F), pale blue grey in reduction, more cream-coloured in oxidation.

Additions

a) With iron oxide 2%, a subtle mid-green celadon develops in reduction, a pale honey in oxidation.

b) With iron oxide 8%, an excellent tenmoku results in reduction, more muted in oxidation.

384 Iron base glaze

Feldspar	40
Whiting	18
Red clay	5
China clay	12
Quartz	25

A smooth clear glaze base, creamy in oxidation, more blue grey in reduction.

Additions

(*a*) With iron oxide 6%, a rich olive green develops in oxidation, more shiny in reduction.

(*b*) With iron oxide 8%, a reddish ochre glaze develops, more brown black in reduction.

(*c*) With iron oxide 12%, a dark red brown develops in oxidation, a rich tenmoku in reduction.

(*d*) With iron oxide 15%, a black red develops in oxidation, a khaki red with iron crystals in reduction.

385 Good clear glaze

Feldspar	50
Whiting	17
Zinc oxide	3
China clay	10
Flint	20

A clear, slightly crackled glaze in oxidation, a more blue grey in reduction.

Additions

(*a*) With iron oxide 2%, a bright green grey celadon on reduction, a pale honey in oxidation.

(*b*) With iron oxide 8%, a rich black tenmoku on stoneware in reduction, a more orange brown in oxidation.

386 Excellent base for iron glazes (reduction)

Feldspar	20
Cornish (Cornwall) stone	50
Whiting	15
Flint	5
China clay	10

A smooth, clear pale grey blue in reduction. The base glaze works well over the slips YS, IS, RS and BS in reduction.

Additions

(*a*) With iron oxide 2%, green and pale green celadon.
(*b*) With iron oxide 8%, gives a good shiny tenmoku.

387 Smooth base glaze, good for iron

Feldspar	55
Whiting	25
Red clay	20

A crazed shiny speckled pale honey in oxidation, a pale grey green in reduction. Excellent iron responses over YS (tenmoku) and IS (green tenmoku) in oxidation. Rich green brown over YS in reduction.

Addition

(*a*) With iron oxide 6%, attractive black brown glaze.

388 Smooth iron base glaze

Cornish (Cornwall) stone	65
Whiting	18
China clay	17

Smooth semi-matt glaze in oxidation and reduction. Rich variety of effects over YS and BS in oxidation and reduction.

Additions

(*a*) With iron oxide 8%, smooth rich semi-matt tenmoku in reduction, rich red brown in oxidation.
(*b*) With iron oxide 2%, soft celadon in reduction, drier lovat green in oxidation.
(*c*) With iron oxide 5%, dark green in reduction, ochre green in oxidation.

389 Iron base glaze (reduction)

Feldspar	75
Whiting	10
Quartz	12
Bentonite	3

An almost colourless stiff base glaze; pale grey in reduction, smooth over BS, IS and YS.

Additions

(*a*) With iron oxide 2%, pale green grey celadon.
(*b*) With iron oxide 5%, dark tenmoku glaze.
(*c*) With iron oxide 8%, classic tenmoku; good over stoneware and porcelain.

4. Decorative and textural glazes

390 A barium carbonate silky matt

Feldspar	55
Barium carbonate	15
Dolomite	5
Nepheline syenite	5
China clay	10
Flint	10

A smooth silky barium carbonate matt glaze.

Addition

(*a*) With copper carbonate 1.5%, a sea green develops on porcelain; drier on stoneware.

(*b*) With cobalt carbonate 0.5% and rutile 3%, a medium blue develops, more mottled in reduction.

391 Dry speckled matt

Feldspar	50
Whiting	25
Zinc oxide	5
China clay	20

A dry white matt glaze with cream speckles, more blue in reduction.

392 Matt white icing-sugar glaze base

Nepheline syenite	70
Dolomite	3
China clay	10
Barium carbonate	15
Flint	2

A smooth matt glaze with the appearance of icing-sugar. In reduction the glaze is responsive to copper oxide in the atmosphere and takes on pink blushes of colour.

Addition

(*a*) With copper carbonate 1.5%, a dark dusky pink in reduction. In oxidation a drier green breaking yellow where thin.

393 A dry sculptural glaze

Calcium borate frit (P2954) (Colemanite)	3
Feldspar	17
Dolomite	5
Whiting	25
China clay	50

A dry glaze with a chalky mottled appearance, more speckled in reduction. With small additions of colouring oxides, attractive soft colours develop.

Addition

(*a*) With cobalt carbonate 0.25%, rutile 1.5% and copper carbonate 1.5%, a soft mottled pale blue green develops at a wide range of temperatures, darker in reduction.

394 A dry ash glaze

Whiting	5
Soda feldspar	30
Mixed wood ash	35
China clay	30

A dry matt white orange speckle in oxidation, smoother in reduction. Do not apply thickly.

Addition

(*a*) With iron oxide 3%, a red orange speckle in oxidation, smoother in reduction.

395 Ash glaze for slips

Wood ash	20
Soda feldspar	55
Red clay	25

A dry glaze which gives rich mottled effects over slips. In oxidation, a green brown over IS, a spotted black brown over YS (do not apply thickly). In reduction rich brown black over YS, a black green over BS.

396 A mottled ash glaze

Wood ash	45
Barium carbonate	10
Chesterfield clay (Albany slip)	45

A pale yellow orange in oxidation, a greener red in reduction. A rich tenmoku over IS in reduction.

Additions

(*a*) With iron oxide 4%, a rich matt red develops in oxidation, a darker matt in reduction.

(*b*) With cobalt oxide 1%, a mottled dark blue grey on porcelain in oxidation and reduction.

397 Runny ash glaze

Mixed wood ash	80
Feldspar	10
Talc	10

A typical runny mottled ash glaze in oxidation and reduction. Do not overfire. Good iron tenmokus over IS and YS in reduction.

398 Mottled ash type raw glaze

Porcelain body	60
Whiting	40

A raw glaze which is best applied to ware before biscuit firing. An excellent ash type glaze in oxidation, giving a broken, pale creamy matt white. Less attractive in reduction. In oxidation attractive mottled blue (BS), and yellow black (VS). Good iron tenmoku response in reduction from IS and VS.

Addition

Many oxides will work well with this glaze.

(*a*) With iron oxide 2–6%, gives pale cream to ochres in oxidation, more green brown in reduction.

399 A matt reactive glaze

Nepheline syenite	50
Whiting	30
Red clay	20

A matt pale yellow orange in oxidation; a shiny green grey in reduction. In oxidation on GS, a matt blue green speckle, blue green black (BS), yellow red (YS). In reduction a grey matt (RS), black (IS).

400 Shino type glaze

Calcium borate frit (P2954) (Colemanite)	5
Alkaline frit (P2962)	4
Nepheline syenite	55
Spodumene	20
Ball clay	16

A pale clear glaze with orange flashing on stoneware in oxidation; attractive brown and orange speckle on stoneware in reduction. Oil spot effects over YS in oxidation; more orange brown in reduction.

401 Pink green semi-matt glaze

Feldspar	58
Barium carbonate	25
Lithium carbonate	2
Flint	5
China clay	10
+ Copper oxide	1.5

An interesting pink green in reduction with a smooth semi-matt surface; a dry turquoise in oxidation.

1260°–1280°C (2300°–2336°F) Orton cones 8–9

402 Smooth clear glaze

Feldspar	50
Alkaline frit (P2962)	7
Whiting	15
China clay	10
Flint	18

A clear glaze in oxidation, a pale blue grey in reduction. 1280°C (2336°F)

403 Semi-clear

Nepheline syenite	30
Whiting	35
Ball clay	10
Flint	25

A 'chunky' glaze which is semi-crazed. In oxidation gives a white frosty light crackle. In reduction a heavier crackle, pale blue on porcelain, pale green on stoneware. 1280°C (2336°F)

404 Semi-clear transparent

Soda feldspar	42
Quartz	25
Whiting	18
China clay	5

A pale blue white transparent in reduction; a clear, semi-transparent in oxidation.

405 A bright white

Feldspar	38
Cornish (Cornwall) stone	40
Whiting	11
China clay	11
+ Tin oxide	3

A smooth bright white in oxidation and reduction.

406 Semi-opaque glaze

Cornish (Cornwall) stone	35
Nepheline syenite	45
Whiting	10
China clay	10

A stiff satin glaze in reduction, more frosty in oxidation. Pink *sang de boeuf* over GS in reduction, drier orange green in oxidation.

Additions

(*a*) With tin oxide 3%, a smoother white opaque in oxidation at 1200°C (2192°F) and 1260°C (2300°F) on porcelain. More opaque on stoneware.

(*b*) With copper oxide 1%, a matt green brown on porcelain in oxidation, a smooth dark *sang de boeuf* in reduction.

407 Stiff semi-opaque

Cornish (Cornwall) stone	35
Feldspar	45
Dolomite	10
China clay	10

A stiff pale grey blue semi-opaque in reduction, non-matt in oxidation.

Additions

(*a*) With tin oxide 3%, a bright glaze results in reduction.
(*b*) With iron oxide 2%, a pale celadon results in reduction.
(*c*) With iron oxide 6%, a stiff oil spot brown results in oxidation at 1200°C (2193°F) and 1260°C (2300°F).

408 Semi-matt smooth glaze (reduction)

Soda feldspar	65
Whiting	12
Barium carbonate	10
Flint	6
China clay	7

A hard smooth semi-opaque glaze in reduction. Excellent iron response over BS (blue black and grey).

409 Good clear base

Talc	5
Whiting	15
Feldspar	33
Ball clay	11
China clay	10
Flint	26

A smooth clear glaze, creamy in oxidation, pale blue in reduction. Mottled green brown over IS, black brown over YS (apply thinly) in oxidation. Rich iron green over YS in reduction. 1280°C (2336°F).

Additions

(*a*) With iron oxide 2%, a medium dark celadon in reduction, an olive green in oxidation.

(*b*) With iron oxide 8%, good tenmokus result in oxidation and reduction.

410 Shino type glaze

Soda feldspar	15
Nepheline syenite	50
Petalite	12
China clay	18
Red clay	5

A rich opaque white with orange flashing and speckling; best in reduction on stoneware and porcelain. In oxidation the glaze is drier. Excellent orange red browns in reduction, over IS and GS. Dry crawl effects in oxidation, over BS, IS and GS. 1280°C (2336F).

Additions

(*a*) With iron oxide 2%, an opaque orange glaze results; in oxidation, a more orange pinhole surface.

(*b*) With iron oxide 5%, a dark orange brown with oil spotting in oxidation, a burnt brown in reduction.

411 Smooth white (reduction)

Feldspar	20
Alkaline frit (P2962)	5
Dolomite	5
Whiting	15
China clay	10
Flint	45

A hard base glaze in reduction, giving a smooth semi-opaque white with good response over YS. 1280°C (2336°F).

412 Reduction hard semi-shiny clear

Cornish (Cornwall) stone	45
Whiting	6
Dolomite	12
China clay	7
Flint	30

A muted, strong pale blue giving soft greys and greens over YS. 1280°C (2336°F).

List of UK and US materials

The following is a list of the glaze materials used in this book, with American equivalents indicated where necessary.

UK	USA
Alkaline leadless frit P2962 (Potterycrafts Ltd) (BaO 0.105, Na_20 0.58, K_2O 0.21, CaO 0.105, $A1_2O_3$ 0.093, SiO_2 1.660, B_2O_3 0.105)	Ferro 3110 (CaO 6.3, Na_2O 15.3, K_2O 2.3, $A1_2O_3$ 3.7, SiO_2 69.8, B_2O_3 2.6) Frit 386 (Standard Ceramic Supply Co) (SiO_2, 57.41, B_2O_3 8.36, $A1_2O_3$ 4.96, CaO 4.35, Na_2O 4.21, K_2O 2.76, ZnO 10.48, BaO 7.45) Pemco P–991 (SiO_2 51.7, B_2O_3 5, Al_2O_3 13.9, CaO 6.4, Na_2O 9, K_2O 3.7, ZnO 10.3, BaO 7.45)
Ball clay (Hymod SMD)	Kentucky ball clay
Barium carbonate ($BaCO_3$)	Tennessee ball clay
Bentonite	
Bone ash (3CaO. P_2O_5)	
Borax frit P2957 (Potterycrafts Ltd) (CaO 0.594, Na_2O 0.264, K_2O 0.132, $A1_2O_3$ 0.418, SiO_2 4.703, B_2O_3 0.963)	Ferro 3134 (Na_2O 10.3, CaO 20.1, B_2O_3 23.1, SiO_2 46.5) Frit 550 (Standard Ceramic Supply Co) (SiO_2 50.52, B_2O_3 18.69, Al_2O_3 4.99, CaO 16.99, Na_2O 8.80) Pemco P-926 (SiO_2 50.5, B_2O_3 18.7, $A1_2O_3$ 5, CaO 17, Na_2O 8.5, K_2O 0.3) Hommel 14
Calcium borate frit P2954 (Potterycrafts Ltd)	Colmanite; Gerstley borate
Chesterfield clay	Albany clay
China clay ($A1_2$ O_3, $2SiO_2$, $2H_2$ O)	EPK; Forida; Georgia china clay
Chromium oxide (Cr_2 O_3)	
Cobalt carbonate ($CoCO_3$)	
Cobalt oxide (CoO)	
Copper carbonate ($CuCO_3$)	
Copper oxide (CuO)	
Cornish stone (K_2O. $A1_2O_3$. $8SiO_2$) (China stone) (Mineral flux)	Cornwall stone, Carolina stone, Kona A-3 Pyrophyllite
Cryolite (Na_3 $A1F_6$ or 3NaF $A1F_3$)	
Dolomite ($CaCO_3$. $MgCO_3$)	
Feldspar (potash) (K_2 O. $A1_2$ O_3. $6SiO_2$)	Bell, Buckingham G-200, Kingman, K-200, Custer, Clinchfield # 202
Feldspar (soda) (Na_2 O. $A1_2$ O_3.$6SiO_2$)	Spruce Pine 4; Kona F-4
Flint (Quartz) (SiO_2)	
Fluorspar (CaF_2)	
Fremington clay (ball milled for four hours)	Albany slip clay

UK	USA
Ilmenite (Fe_2O_3. TiO_2)	
Iron oxide (Black) (FeO)	
Iron oxide (Red) (Fe_2O_3)	
Lead bisilicate (PbO. $2SiO_2$) (PbO 65, SiO_2 32.2, $A1_2O_3$ 2.8)	Ferro 3498 (PbO 65.3, $A1_2O_3$ 6.2, SiO_2 32.2) O Hommel 14 Frit 28 (Standard Ceramic Supply Co) (Pbo 65, SiO_2 34, $A1_2O_3$ 1) Pemco Pb-700 (PbO 65, SiO_2 34, $A1_2O_3$ 1)
Lepidolite $(LiK)_2$. $(FOH)_2$. $A1_2O_3$. 3Sio$_2$)	
Lithium carbonate (Li_2CO_3)	
Manganese carbonate ($MnCO_3$)	
Manganese oxide (MnO)	
Nepheline syenite (K_2O. $3Na_2O$ 4 $A1_2O_3$. $8SiO_2$)	
Nickel oxide (NiO)	
Petalite (LiO. $A1_2O_3$. $8SiO_2$)	
Rutile ($FeTiO_3$)	
Silicon carbide (SiC) (Fine) Carborundum)	
Spodumene (LiO_2. $A1_2O_3$. $4SiO_2$)	
Talc ($3MgO$. $4SiO_2$)	
Tin oxide (SnO_2)	
Titanium oxide (TiO_2)	
Uranium oxide (U_2O_8)	
Vanadium pentoxide (V_2O_5)	
Volcanic ash (Pumice)	
Whiting ($CaCO_3$)	
Wollastonite (CaO. SiO_2)	'Opax', 'Superpax', 'Zircopax'
Wood ash (mixed)	
Yellow ochre (Fe_2O_3. H_2O)	
Zinc oxide (ZnO)	
Zirconium silicate ($ZrSiO_4$) (Zircon) ('Disperson')	

Conversion tables

Temperature conversion

°Centigrade	°Fahrenheit	°Centigrade	°Fahrenheit
1	33.8	90	194
2	35.6	100	212
3	37.4	200	392
4	39.2	300	572
5	41.0	400	752
6	42.8	500	932
7	44.6	600	1112
8	46.4	700	1292
9	48.2	800	1472
10	50	900	1652
20	68	1000	1832
30	86	1100	2012
40	104	1200	2192
50	122	1220	2228
60	140	1300	2372
70	158	1400	2552
80	176	1500	2732

To convert °C into °F multiply by 1.8 and add 32.
To convert °F into °C multiply by 0.55 and subtract 32.

Conversion table for pyrometric cones

°C	°F	*British Cones*	*Seger Cones*	*Orton Cones*
950	1742	—	—	08
960	1760	07	07a	—
970	1778	—	—	17
980	1796	06	06a	—
985	1805	—	—	—
990	1814	—	—	07
1000	1832	05	05a	—
1015	1859	—	—	06
1020	1868	04	04a	—
1030	1886	—	—	—
1040	1904	03	03a	05
1060	1940	02	02a	04
1065	1949	—	—	—
1080	1976	01	01a	—
1100	2012	1	1a	—
1115	2039	—	—	03
1120	2048	2	2a	—
1125	2057	—	—	02
1135	2075	—	—	—
1140	2084	3	3a	—
1145	2093	—	—	01
1190	2174	—	—	4
1200	2192	6	6a	—
1205	2201	—	—	5
1230	2246	7	7	6
1240	2264	—	—	—
1250	2282	8	8	7
1260	2300	8a	—	8
1270	2318	—	—	—
1275	2327	—	—	—
1280	2336	9	9	—
1285	2345	—	—	9
1300	2372	10	10	—
1305	2381	—	—	10

The relationship between temperature and cones is a function of time and temperature.
For standard size cones, the squatting temperature depends on the rate of firing. When Orton Cones are heated at 150°C (302°F) per hour the above equivalents are approximately correct. With slower rates of firing, cones will be affected at lower temperatures. Actual temperatures are determined by accurately calibrated pyrometers.

Further reading

Books

COOPER, E. and ROYLE, D., *Glazes for the Studio Potter,* Batsford, London; Scribner, New York. A readable and thorough explanation of how glazes are made and applied from start to finish.

COOPER, E., *Electric Kiln Pottery,* Batsford, London. A clear and comprehensive account of working with electric kilns.

GREEN, D., *A Handbook of Pottery Glazes,* Faber & Faber, London. A comprehensive discussion on glaze construction and ceramic science.

PARMELEE, C. W., *Ceramic Glazes,* Chaners Books. A scientific and detailed explanation of how to make commercial glazes.

WOOD, N., *Oriental Glazes,* Pitman, London; Watson-Guptill, New York. A potter's look at how the classical Chinese glazes can be made.

Magazines

UK

Ceramic Review 21 Carnaby Street, London W1V 1PH

USA

Ceramics Monthly 1609 Northwest Blvd, Box 12448, Columbus, Ohio 43212
American Ceramics 9 East 45 Street, New York NY 10017
Studio Potter Box 65, Goffstown, NH 03045

AUSTRALIA

Pottery in Australia 2/68 Alexander Street, Crows Nest, NSW 2065
Ceramics: Art and Perception 35 William Street, Paddington, NSW 2021

NEW ZEALAND

The New Zealand Potter P.O. Box 147, Albany

Suppliers

UK

Raw materials, frits, kilns, clays etc

Potclays Ltd
Brickkiln Lane
Etruria
Stoke-on-Trent
ST1 4PQ

Fulham Pottery
8-10 Ingate Place
London SW8 3NS

Potterycrafts Ltd
Campbell Road
Stoke-on-Trent ST4 4ET

Ferro (Great Britain) Ltd
Ounsdale Road
Wombourne
Wolverhampton WV5 8DA

Stanton Pottery Supplies Ltd
Canal Lane
Westport Lake
Tunstall
Stoke-on-Trent ST6 4NZ

Degg Industrial Minerals Ltd
Phoenix Works
Webberley Lane
Longton
Stoke-on-Trent ST3 1RJ

Cromartie Kilns Ltd
Park Hall Road
Longton
Stoke-on-Trent ST3 5AY

Kilns & Furnaces Ltd
Keele Street
Stoke-on-Trent ST6 5AS

Laser Kilns Ltd
Unit 9, Crispin Industrial Centre
Angel Road Works
London N18 2DT

Creative Ceramics Ltd
Whitebridge Industrial Estate
Whitebridge Lane
Stone, Staffordshire

Clay

Fremington Red Earthenware Clay
C. H. Brannam, Litchdon Potteries,
Barnstaple, Devon

Chesterfield clay

John Winter and Co
Washer Lane Works, PO Box 21, Halifax
Halifax HX2 7DP

Chemical suppliers

BDH Chemicals Ltd
Poole, Dorset BH12 4NN

Hopkin and Williams
Freshwater Road, Chadwell Heath, Essex
PO Box 1, Romford RM1 1HA

Depleted uranium U_3O_8

British Nuclear Fuels, Risley,
Warrington, Lancs

Laboratories which will test for metal release

Harrison Mayer Ltd
Uttoxeter Road
Meir
Stoke-on-Trent

British Ceramic Research Association
Queens Road
Penkhull, Stoke-on-Trent

Ellis Testing and Research Laboratory
Aldbury
Nr Guildford, Surrey

USA

American Art Clay Co (Amaco)
4177 West 16th Street
Indianapolis Ind 46222

Westwood Ceramic Supply Company
14400 Lomitas Avenue
City of Industry
Calif 91744

B. F. Drakenfeld and Co Inc
Washington PA 15301

Hammill and Gillespie, Inc
225 Broadway
New York NY 10007

Pemco Products Group
5601 Eastern Avenue
Baltimore
Maryland 21224

Leslie Ceramic Supply, Co
1212 San Pablo Avenue
Berkeley, CA 94706

Standard Ceramic Supply Company
Box 4435
Pittsburgh, PA 15205

Rovin Ceramics
6912 Schaefer Road
Dearborn, MI 48126

Cedar Heights Clay Company
50 Portsmouth Road
Oak Hill, OH 45656

Ferro Corporation
4150 East 56th Street
Cleveland, Ohio 44101

Harrison Bell (associate company of Harrison Mayer Ltd)
3605A Kennedy Road
South Plainfield
New Jersey

The O Hommel Company
PO Box 475
Pittsburgh
Pennsylvania 15230

Laboratories which will test for metal release

Pittsburgh Testing Laboratory
850 Poplar Street
Pittsburgh, PA 15220

Bio-Technics Laboratories, Inc
1133 Crenshaw Blvd.
Los Angeles, CA 90019

The Twining Laboratories, Inc
Box 1472
Fresno, CA 93716

Coors Spectro-Chemical Laboratory
Box 500
Golden, CO 80401

CANADA

Pottery Supply House
PO Box 192
2070 Speers Road
Oakville, Ontario

Ferro Enamels (Canada) Ltd
354 Davis
Oakville, Ontario

Index to glaze recipes—materials, colour and types

This index includes particular glaze materials which have a major influence on the glaze (i.e. barium carbonate) but excludes common ingredients such as feldspars which occur in practically every recipe. Colour responses and glaze types enable particular effects to be found quickly. Colour descriptions include a range of tones and shades, and testing is necessary to observe precise effects. 'Greens', for example, include olive, holly, lovat, pale and pea green.

Each entry is divided into eight sections denoted by Roman numerals. These correspond with the eight groups classified according to the firing temperature of the glaze:

I 1060°–1080°C (1940°–1976°F)
II 1060°–1150°C (1940°–2093°F)
III 1150°–1200°C (2093°–2192°F)
IV 1200°C (2192°F)
V 1200°–1220°C (2192°–2228°F)
VI 1200°–1260°C (2192°–2300°F)
VII 1260°C (2300°F)
VIII 1260°–1280°C (2300°–2336°F)

Entries which stop short of eight sections (e.g. Adventurine, with only I) means that the ingredient does not occur in any sections after those indicated.